MW01120615

Criminal Justice, Law Enforcement and Corrections Series

# INCARCERATION AND THE FAMILY: ISSUES, EFFECTS AND APPROACHES TO SUCCESSFUL REENTRY

# CRIMINAL JUSTICE, LAW ENFORCEMENT AND CORRECTIONS SERIES

**Homicide Investigations**
*Allan B. Smythe (Editor)*
2009 ISBN 978-1-60692-258-3

**Mass Incarceration and Offender Registry in the United States**
*Russell D. Javitze (Editor)*
2009 ISBN 978-1-60692-657-4

**Batterer Intervention:**
**Program Approaches and Criminal Justice Strategies**
*Kerry Healey, Christine Smith and Chris O'Sullivan*
2009 ISBN 978-1-60692-934-6

**Digital Surveillance: Laws, Security and Related Issues**
*Joseph G. Massingale (Editor)*
2009 ISBN 978-1-60692-312-2

**Incarceration and the Family: Issues, Effects and Approaches to Successful Reentry**
*United States Department of Health and Human Services*
2009. ISBN 978-1-60692-933-9

Criminal Justice, Law Enforcement and Corrections Series

# INCARCERATION AND THE FAMILY: ISSUES, EFFECTS AND APPROACHES TO SUCCESSFUL REENTRY

## U.S. DEPARTMENT OF HEALTH AND HUMAN SERVICES

Nova Science Publishers, Inc.

*New York*

For permission to use material from this book please contact us:
Telephone 631-231-7269; Fax 631-231-8175
Web Site: http://www.novapublishers.com

### NOTICE TO THE READER

LIBRARY OF CONGRESS CATALOGING-IN-PUBLICATION DATA

*Available upon request*

ISBN: 978-1-60692-933-9

*Published by Nova Science Publishers, Inc.* ✛ *New York*

# CONTENTS

# PREFACE[*]

This book provides an overview of the current research that addresses issues concerning incarcerated men, their partner and parenting relationships, and the policies and programs that may assist them in their rehabilitation in prison and after release. The number of individuals involved in the criminal justice system is at an historic high. More stringent sentencing standards for felons, harsher laws on drug-related activity, and more aggressive prosecution practices have combined to bring an unprecedented number of Americans under correctional supervision. Over the last 25 years, the number of incarcerated persons has increased four-fold. Most individuals leave behind intimate partners and children when they go to prison, and this separation can have negative repercussions on family life.

Examined in this book are social policies that address intersection of incarceration and family life that have emerged at federal, state, and local levels.

This book consists of public domain documents which have been located, gathered, combined, reformatted, and enhanced with a subject index, perhaps edited and bound to provide easy access.

---

[*] This is an edited, excerpted and augmented edition of a U.S. Department of Health and Human Services publication, dated September 2008.

# ACKNOWLEDGMENTS

We would like to express our gratitude to Amy Sullivan for assistance with references, and to Christopher Mumola and Jacinta Bronte-Tinkew for providing us with unpublished material from their research.

This report was prepared by RTI International for the Office of the Assistant Secretary for Planning and Evaluation, Office of the Secretary, and the Office of Family Assistance, Administration for Children and Families, United States Department of Health and Human Services, under Contract Number HHSP23320062920YC, September 2006. The views, opinions and findings expressed in this document are those of the report authors and the researchers whose work was included in the review and do not necessarily represent the official positions and policies of the United States Department of Health and Human Services.

# SUMMARY POINTS

- The number of individuals involved in the criminal justice system is at a historic high. There are almost 2.3 million individuals in U.S. jails and prisons and more than 798,000 people on parole. It is estimated that 7,476,500 children have a parent who is in prison, in jail or under correctional supervision.
- Minority children are disproportionately affected by father imprisonment: In state prisons, 42% of fathers are African American, and African American children are seven and a half times more likely to have a parent in prison than white children (6.7% vs. 0.9%).
- Only 23% of state prisoners are married, but many are involved in intimate or co-parenting relationships.
- Father incarceration negatively affects family life. Spouses/partners face serious financial strains, social isolation and stigma, loneliness, and negative emotions such as anger and resentment.
- Children of incarcerated fathers also may experience numerous life stressors, including caregiver changes, increased poverty, and involvement with the child welfare system, in addition to the pain of parental separation. These stressors have been linked to increased rates of anxiety, depression, learning problems, and aggression.
- Fathers in prison face a host of problems that limit their ability to be successful at reentry including substance abuse, mental illness, low educational attainment, and poor employment histories.
- Most men plan to live with their families upon release, and those who report positive family and parenting relationships during reentry are less likely to recidivate. Family support services during incarceration and after release are an important strategy for increasing criminal desistance,

yet family strengthening services are often a neglected aspect of rehabilitation.

- Marriage and relationship enhancement interventions in prison show promise in reducing negative interactions and in improving communication skills and relationship satisfaction.

- Findings from evaluations of parenting programs in prison also are encouraging: inmates involved in such programs indicate improved attitudes about the importance of fatherhood, increased parenting skills, and more frequent contact with their children.

- To be successful, family strengthening services for prisoners require coordination between criminal justice and human service agencies, which often have divergent goals and contrasting perspectives. Success is also tied to effective linkages between prisons and community partners.

- Obstacles to family strengthening efforts during incarceration and re-entry include distance between place of imprisonment and reentry community, difficulties in recruiting and retaining prisoners, inhospitable visiting rules, unsupportive extended family relations, and barriers to partner and child involvement such as transportation difficulties, busy schedules, and relationship strain.

- The evidence for marital partner education and parenting programs is just beginning to accumulate. This evidence is hampered by a lack of rigorous evaluation methods. Studies have rarely employed randomized controlled trials, which are the gold standard for program evaluation. Program assessments also have had limited follow-ups to assess the maintenance of behavioral change and frequently rely on non-standardized measures and self-reports to document change.

- Effective social policies are critical for reducing recidivism and decreasing the negative effects of incarceration on children and families.

# Chapter 1

# POLICY BACKGROUND

The number of individuals involved in the criminal justice system is at a historic high. More stringent sentencing standards for felons, harsher laws on drug-related activity, and more aggressive prosecution practices have combined to bring an unprecedented number of Americans under correctional supervision (Western & McLenahan, 2000; Hagan & Dinovitzer, 1999; Western & Beckett, 1999). Over the last 25 years, the number of incarcerated persons has increased four-fold (Baer et al., 2005). As of June 2007, there were 2,299,116 people incarcerated in federal and state prisons and local jails. An additional 4,237,000 persons were on probation and another 798,200 were on parole. The number of sentenced prisoners per 100,000 U.S. residents increased from 501 to 509 between year-end 2006 and midyear 2007 (Bureau of Justice Statistics, 2008). Most individuals leave behind intimate partners and children when they go to prison, and this separation can have negative repercussions on family life.

> *There are almost 2.3 million individuals in U.S. jails and prisons and more than 798,000 people on parole.*

Social policies that address the intersection of incarceration and family life have emerged at the federal, state, and local levels. Family strengthening policies, including the federal Healthy Marriage and Responsible Fatherhood grants administered by the Department of Health and Human Services, are supported by research indicating the benefits of healthy relationships and involved fatherhood. Happily married individuals are more likely to report good physical and psychological health than unmarried persons. They also are more likely to be positively engaged in work and other productive activities and are less likely to smoke, drink heavily, and be physically inactive compared with their unmarried counterparts (Schoenborn, 2004). A good marriage is even associated with greater happiness, life satisfaction, and longevity (Coombs, 1991; Seeman, 1996).

Stable parental relationships also confer many advantages to children: Children residing in households with two married, biologic or adoptive parents show superior outcomes in socioemotional adjustment and academic achievement compared with children from single-or step-parent households (Mosley & Thomson, 1995; Nord, Brimhall, & West, 1997). Children growing up in families with healthy marriages are, on average, more likely to report positive mental and physical health, avoid drugs and alcohol, do well in school, and go to college. They are less likely to experience poverty, suffer physical and sexual abuse, and develop emotional or behavioral problems (Amato, 2005; Doherty & Anderson, 2004; Parke, 2003). Research indicates that two-parent families may help promote child resilience by providing a higher standard of living, offering more effective parenting strategies, and decreasing children's exposure to stressful circumstances. Thus, healthy relationship and family strengthening policies may be one route for reducing child poverty and enhancing child wellbeing (Family Strengthening Policy Center, 2005).

Concurrent with the development of family strengthening programs, criminal justice policy has increasingly promoted "second chance" initiatives for incarcerated men and women upon release. One example of such a policy is the Department of Justice's Serious and Violent Offender Re-entry Initiative (SVORI), which in 2003 funded states and local communities to develop educational programs, training, and reentry strategies to reduce recidivism and promote healthy outcomes, including strong marriages, for ex-offenders. The Department of Labor's Prison Reentry Initiative (PRI) of 2004 also expanded reentry supports for newly released prisoners by funding local faith- and community-based organizations to offer housing, employment and mentoring programs to releasees (Department of Labor, 2007). Research reveals that partners of incarcerated men face financial strains and emotional difficulties. Moreover, children of incarcerated parents face a higher risk of experiencing poverty as well as social, emotional, and learning problems (Parke & Clarke-Stewart, 2001). However, incarcerated men and their families rarely receive family strengthening programs despite research that indicates that positive family relationships are linked with lower rates of recidivism (Visher & Travis, 2003).

Recognizing a joint policy issue for the human services and criminal justice community, the Office of the Assistant Secretary for Planning and Evaluation

(ASPE), in collaboration with the Substance Abuse and Mental Health Services Administration (SAMHSA) and the National Institute for Child Health and Human Development (NICHD), convened an expert panel in 2002 concerning the effect of incarceration on children and families. Summary findings from this panel reveal the dearth of research on family issues among incarcerated individuals. They point to large research gaps including little understanding of the needs of families with an incarcerated father, what works to promote healthy relationship skills and positive parenting among incarcerated men, and how to deliver and evaluate family strengthening programs within the criminal justice system (Festen, Waul, Solomon & Travis, 2002).

Motivated by the increasing number of imprisoned parents and the lack of focus on family relationships in existing reentry programs and policies (Day, Acock, Bahr & Arditti, 2005), HHS established, as a priority area under the Healthy Marriage Promotion and Responsible Fatherhood provisions of the Deficit Reduction Act of 2005 (P.L. 109-171), Marriage, and Family Strengthening Grants for Incarcerated Fathers and Their Partners (MFS-IP). MFS-IP's overarching goal is to enhance marital relations and parenting skills among men currently incarcerated or under criminal justice supervision. This resource document provides an overview of the current research underlying MFS-IP and addresses issues concerning incarcerated men, their partner and parenting relationships, and the policies and programs that may assist them in their rehabilitation in prison and after release.

## 1.1. MARRIAGE AND CRIMINAL DESISTANCE

One rationale for providing marriage education to criminal offenders is research indicating that marriage plays an important role in criminal desistance (Sampson, Laub, & Wimer, 2006). The classic study *Unraveling Juvenile Delinquency* (Glueck & Glueck, 1950) found that marriage is a key turning point in individuals' lives and helped promote lawful and responsible adult behavior. Laub and colleagues (1998) analyzed data from 500 delinquent boys followed from 1940 to 1965. Using multiple methods such as personal and key informant interviews, they found that individuals who were able to maintain good marriages over time were 68% less likely to commit criminal offenses as adults. More recent data from the Returning Home project bears out the association between criminal desistance and involvement in healthy committed relationships. Analyzing data on criminal activity and drug use in a subsample of 652 released men returning to three U.S. cities, Visher et al., (forthcoming) found that men who were married or in committed cohabiting relationships were half as likely to report engaging in drug use and/or committing a new crime at eight months post-release compared to those who were uninvolved or in non-committed relationships. The association remained even after controlling analytically for selection into intimate relationships.

> *Marriage is a key turning point in individuals' lives and helps promote lawful and responsible adult behavior.*

Sampson, Laub, and Wimer (2006) theorize that the social bonds created through marriage may help limit criminal activity through several mechanisms: (1) Marriage creates interdependence and role obligations that extract a high social cost if broken. (2) Marriage leads to changes in day-to-day routines and affiliations. Married men, and especially those who are also parents, have less opportunity to spend time with deviant peers. (3) Wives exert some level of social control over their husbands, limiting and structuring their social life. (4) Marriage may lead to changes in self-perceptions as in the need to "grow up and get serious."

Research suggests that it is the quality of marriage, not the event itself, which buffers men from criminal involvement. Using the same data set, Sampson and Laub (1990) found that the quality of marital attachment at age 25 to 32 was a significant predictor of future criminal behavior. Thus, intervention efforts to enhance the quality of the marital bond may be an important way to decrease criminal behavior and recidivism. However, many historical and cultural changes have occurred since this study was conducted, and new research is needed to corroborate these findings.

## 1.2. PURPOSE OF THIS REPORT

In order to develop effective family strengthening programs and policies, we need a better understanding of the characteristics of incarcerated individuals, their partner and parenting relationships, and the processes through which imprisonment and reentry may undermine these attachments. This document is intended to be such a resource for the field. We begin in Chapter 2 by describing men in prison, including their sociodemographics, marital and parenting status, and criminal justice characteristics. In Chapter 3, we discuss the effects of incarceration on marriage and partner relationships. Chapter 4 focuses on the effect incarceration has on children. In Chapter 5, we address the challenges of reentry on the marital/partner relationship, and issues concerning the father- child relationship at reentry are presented in Chapter 6. In Chapter 7 we describe programs designed to strengthen families both in prison and after release, before going on to discuss the challenges of implementing such programs in Chapter 8. Finally, we close with a summary of the state of the field in Chapter 9.

# Chapter 2

# CHARACTERISTICS OF INCARCERATED FATHERS

## 2.1. PREVALENCE AND SOCIODEMOGRAPHICS

Accurate understanding of the characteristics of fathers involved in the criminal justice system will improve service system planning and delivery. In this chapter we describe the sociodemographic, parenting, sentencing, and health characteristics of incarcerated fathers.

According to the Bureau of Justice Statistics, in 2007 an estimated 744,200 state and federal prisoners in the United States were fathers to 1,599,200 children under the age of 18 (Glaze & Maruschak, 2008). An unpublished estimate from Mumola suggests that 7,476,500 children have a parent (mother or father) who is in prison, in jail or under correctional supervision (2006). Few studies have attempted to describe the characteristics of incarcerated fathers and the children they parent. "Parents in Prison and their Minor Children," a special report from the Bureau of Justice Statistics, is the most complete resource available to date for such information. The report (Glaze & Maruschak, 2008) is based on findings from the Surveys of Inmates in State and Federal Correctional Facilities conducted in 2004, and on National Prisoners Statistics program custody counts. The Surveys of Inmates involved quantitative data collection with a representative sample of 18,185 persons incarcerated in state and federal prisons. We provide some descriptive information about parents in prison, based primarily on this work and its antecedent (Mumola, 2000).

---

> *There are approximately 7.4 million children who have a parent in prison, in jail, or under correctional supervision.*

---

- Of the total number of parents in federal prison, 36% were married and 25% were divorced or separated. Among state prisoners, 23% of parents were married and 28% were divorced or separated (Mumola, 2000).
- Of the state and federal prisoners who had minor children in 2004, 92% were men (Glaze & Maruschak, 2008).
- Over half of incarcerated fathers (54%) reported that they were the primary source of financial support for their children prior to their incarceration (Glaze and Maruschak, 2008).
- In 1997, most incarcerated fathers reported incomes below the poverty line prior to incarceration, with 53% earning less than $12,000 in the year before their arrest (Mumola, 2000).
- Among male inmates in state prison, 71% of those who were married were parents to minor children, compared to 44% of those who were never married, 55% of those who were divorced, and 64% of those who were legally separated. Among federal inmates, 77% of married men had minor children, compared to 58% of never-married men, 59% of divorced men, and 69% of men who were separated (Glaze & Maruschak, 2008).
- In a sample of inmates returning to Cleveland, Ohio, after incarceration, Visher and Courtney (2007) found that 46% had lived with a spouse or intimate partner prior to incarceration.
- The median age of incarcerated parents was 32 among those in state facilities and 35 among those in federal facilities in 1997 (Mumola, 2000).
- In 2007, a disproportionate number of fathers incarcerated in state prison were African American (42%) or Latino (20%). African American (49%) and Latino (28%) men made up a disproportionate share of fathers in federal prison as well (Glaze and Maruschak, 2008).

The percent of male inmates who were fathers, by age group, is shown in Exhibit 2-1.

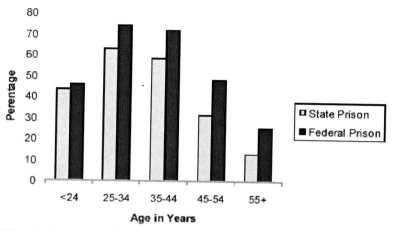

Source: Glaze & Maruschak. (2008). Parents in prison and their minor children. *Bureau of Justice Statistics Special Report.* Washington, DC: Bureau of Justice Statistics.

Exhibit 2-1. Percent Fathers by Age.

## 2.2. PARENTING

The average incarcerated father has 2.1 children. Their parenting relationships are often complex, with some men having children with multiple partners. Forty-two percent of state prisoners reported living with one or more of their minor children in the period immediately prior to their incarceration (Glaze & Maruschak, 2008).

- The average age of children with an incarcerated parent is 8 years old (Mumola, 2000).
- Most incarcerated fathers (88%) report that at least one of their children is in the care of the child's other parent, compared to 37% of mothers (Glaze and Maruschak, 2008).
- Of children with an incarcerated father, 12% live with a grandparent or other relative and 4% live in foster care or with a non-family member (Johnson, 2006).

Exhibit 2-2 shows the percentage of children of incarcerated fathers, by age

| Age | Age Breakdown of Children with Father in Prison |
|---|---|
| Less than 1 year | 2.1% |
| 1–4 years | 20.4% |
| 5–9 years | 35.1% |
| 10–14 years | 28.0% |
| 15–17 years | 14.5% |

Source: Mumola, C. (2000). Incarcerated parents and children. *Bureau of Justice Statistics Special Report.* Washington, DC: Bureau of Justice Statistics.

Exhibit 2-2. Age Breakdown of Children with Fathers in Prison.

## 2.3. TYPE OF OFFENSES

In 2000, 23% of incarcerated fathers were in prison for a first- time offense (Mumola, 2000). Nonviolent offenders, particularly drug offenders, make up an increasing proportion of the U.S. correctional population and are heavily represented among incarcerated parents (Western & Beckett, 1999; Mumola, 2000). Exhibit 2-3 shows the types of offenses committed by fathers in prison.

## 2.4. SENTENCE LENGTH

The most recent published estimates for average sentence length for incarcerated fathers are from the Mumola (2000) report, "Incarcerated Parents and their Children." Average sentence length for fathers was 6 to 7 years among state inmates and 8 to 9 years among federal inmates as of the 1997 data collection on which this report is based.

As shown in Exhibit 2-4, slightly more than half of incarcerated fathers were expected to spend at least 4 years in prison.

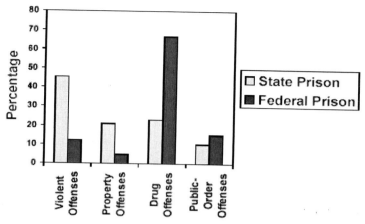

Source: Glaze & Maruschak. (2008). Parents in prison and their minor children. Bureau of Justice Statistics Special Report. Washington, DC: Bureau of Justice Statistics.
Note: Estimates may not sum to 100 due to rounding.

Exhibit 2-3. Types of Offenses Committed by Fathers in Prison.

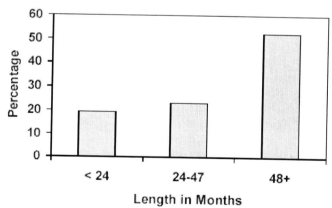

Source: Mumola, C. (2000). Incarcerated parents and their children. *Bureau of Justice Statistics Special Report.* Washington, DC: Bureau of Justice Statistics.

Exhibit 2-4. Sentence Lengths among Fathers in Prison.

A 2006 (unpublished) estimate from Mumola suggests that sentence length characteristics remained relatively unchanged as of the 2004 Surveys of Inmates, with fathers incarcerated in state prison expected to serve an average sentence of six years and ten months. Eighteen percent of fathers were expected to serve less than two years (Mumola, 2006).

- Most parents in state (62%) and federal (84%) prison were being held at correctional facilities located more than 100 miles from their last place of residence prior to incarceration (Mumola, 2000).
- Of parents in federal prison, 43% were held more than 500 miles from their last place of residence, compared with 11% of those in state facilities (Mumola, 2000).

## 2.5. SUBSTANCE ABUSE AND MENTAL HEALTH

Substance abuse and mental health issues are common among incarcerated parents:

- Of parents in state prison in 2004, 58% of fathers and 65% of mothers reported illicit drug use in the month prior to their arrest (Mumola, 2006).
- Based on the DSM-IV criteria, 67% of fathers incarcerated in state prison reported alcohol or drug dependence or abuse prior to arrest (Glaze and Maruschak, 2008).
- One-third of fathers in state prison committed their offense while under the influence of illicit drugs. Thirty- seven percent of fathers in state prison committed their offense while under the influence of alcohol (Mumola, 2006).
- Parents in prison reported slightly higher problems with substance abuse than did non-parents in prison (Mumola, 2006).
- Of fathers classified as having an alcohol or drug use problem, 42% reported having received any substance abuse treatment since admission for the current incarceration (Glaze and Maruschak, 2008).

Mental health issues also plague many incarcerated parents; 49% of fathers in state prison reported clinically meaningful symptoms of mental illness, as did 38% of fathers in federal prison (Glaze & Maruschak, 2008). In general, rates of mental illness among inmates are two to four times higher than among the general population (Lurigio, 2001).

The intergenerational influences of family involvement in prison are strong. Forty-nine percent of fathers in state prison reported that a member of their family (a parent, sibling, or spouse) had ever been incarcerated. Nineteen percent of fathers in state prison had experienced paternal incarceration and 6% had experienced maternal incarceration (Glaze and Maruschak, 2008).

These descriptive statistics reveal the need for comprehensive services to prepare men for release, including relationship and parenting programs and other rehabilitation services to address substance abuse, mental health, and employment problems which may exacerbate family problems and increase risk for recidivism.

## 2.6. RESEARCH LIMITATIONS

Findings from the Surveys of Inmates in State and Federal Correctional Facilities and the National Prisoners Statistics program construct a basic picture of the characteristics of fathers incarcerated in U.S. prisons. Far less is known about fathers in the jail population, however. Given the large number of inmates held in local jails (780,581 as of midyear 2007), preliminary research on their fatherhood status and other characteristics is warranted (BJS, 2008).

The relationships of incarcerated and recently-released men and their current and past partners, are also not well documented. Regional findings from the Returning Home project represent a step toward generating a more complete picture of the family lives of these men, but national research is needed on fathers' relationships and living arrangements prior to, during and after incarceration. In addition, information about these men's attitudes toward, and concerns about, their romantic and parenting relationships is crucial for understanding the needs of these fathers and their families.

# THE EFFECTS OF INCARCERATION ON INTIMATE PARTNER RELATIONSHIPS

## 3.1. Decreased Likelihood of Marriage and Family Involvement

Chapter 3 focuses on the mechanisms through which incarceration takes a toll on intimate relations by reducing men's opportunities for marriage and creating barriers to intimacy, family involvement, and economic contribution.

> *Incarceration is a profoundly stressful event that significantly affects the prisoner, his partner, and his children.*

Incarceration greatly reduces the likelihood that men and women will marry. Analysis of data from both the National Longitudinal Survey of Youth (NLSY) and the Fragile Families and Child Well-being Study indicates that men with a history of incarceration are much less likely to marry compared with men with no incarceration history (Western, Lopoo, & McLanahan, 2004). Huebner (2005) analyzed a subsample of 4,591 adult men who were interviewed 15 times between 1983 and 2000. Using hierarchical linear modeling, she estimated that current incarceration reduced the likelihood of marriage by 39% and prior incarceration reduced the likelihood by 8%. Huebner's (2007) analysis of the same dataset found that incarceration had a differential effect on marriage likelihood by race. Incarceration was associated with a 59% decrease in likelihood of marriage among whites, compared to 30% among African Americans and 41% among Latinos.

Western and McLanahan (2000) explored incarceration and marriage likelihood using data from the Fragile Families and Child Well-being Study. Their analyses were based on 400 mothers and fathers interviewed in Oakland, California, and Austin, Texas. They found that men who had never been incarcerated were twice as likely to marry compared with exinmates (Western & McLanahan, 2000). In addition, ex-inmates were 50% less likely to be involved with their child's mother one year after their child's birth (Western & McLanahan, 2000). Incarceration history decreased the odds of cohabitation by 70% per self-reports from interviewed women. This relationship is especially pronounced for African American families (Western & McLanahan, 2000). Only 8% of African American men with a prior incarceration were married to their partner a year after the birth of their child. Incarceration is estimated to account for 15% of absentee African American fathers (Western & McLanahan, 2000; Western, 2004).

> *By age 40, approximately 87% of nonoffending men were married compared with only 40% of men with a history of incarceration.*

Using NLSY data, Western (2004) analyzed the marriage rates of men from ages 18 to 40. He found that by age 26, 46% of men with no criminal history were married, while this was true of only 25% of men who had been involved in the penal system. The gap widened as men aged: by age 40, approximately 87% of nonoffending men were married compared with only 40% of men with a history of incarceration.

Western (2004) posited that several mechanisms are responsible for the low marriage rate among ex-inmates: incapacitation, stigma, and economic disadvantage. Incapacitation refers to men's inability to meet women as a result of being incarcerated, as well as the constraints placed on inmates' ability to form intimate bonds both during and after release. In addition, the desirability of ex-inmates as marital partners is often decreased by the stigma associated with their criminal histories. Ethnographic interviews with low-income women in Philadelphia suggest that a woman's decision to marry is partly based on her perception of her partner's social respectability and trustworthiness—characteristics often found to be lacking in men with a history of incarceration (Edin, 2000).

Incarceration also diminishes the likelihood of marriage because of the poor economic prospects of ex-inmates. Incarceration has a large negative effect on men's employability. A history of incarceration reduces wages, increases the risk for unemployment, and decreases job stability (Western, 2004). Analyses of the NLSY indicate that incarceration is associated with a 66% decline in employment (Huebner, 2005), and many men released from prison struggle with finding stable employment because of their low education and job skills, as well as discrimination by employers (Visher & Travis, 2003). Poor economic prospects have a significant dampening effect on marriage, as most couples desire financial stability before commitment (Gibson-Davis, Edin, & McLanahan, 2005).

The risk of divorce is also very high for those with an incarceration history. Married men in prison reach the national 50% divorce rate much more quickly than do men in the general population (Western, 2004).

# 3.2. IMPACT OF IMPRISONMENT ON INTIMACY AND COMMITMENT

It is difficult to carry out intimate relationships from prison. Barriers to contact and communication, transformations in family roles, and psychological changes due to detainment impede the development and maintenance of intimacy and commitment.

---

*Limited visiting hours, lack of privacy, and restrictions on movement and physical contact diminish the efforts men and women make to stay connected.*

---

## 3.2.1. Barriers to Contact and Communication

Many prisoners are housed far away from their families. The cost of visitation and the inhospitable prison environment may further inhibit efforts to maintain contact. Limited visiting hours, lack of privacy, and restrictions on movement and physical contact diminish the efforts men and women do make to stay connected (Fishman, 1990; Hairston, Rollin, & Jo, 2004). In interviews with 51 men in minimum security prison in Utah and Oregon, 65% of the men reported that they received no visits from their spouse or partner while in prison (Day et al., 2005).

The limited time for visitation can place undue pressure on what needs to be accomplished during these brief episodes of communication. Fishman (1990) sheds light on the range and intensity of emotions felt during these visits. Women reported feelings of intense anger, attachment, remorse, and resentment, as well as vicious fighting and passionate reconciliation. Fishman conducted repeated qualitative interviews with 65 men and 30 of their wives in prison in Vermont to examine the effect of incarceration on men and their families. She found that women's experiences during visitation varied widely. Some perceived visits as opportunities for renewed courtship, while others found the visits to be stressful and unfulfilling. In many cases, the relationship felt one-sided to the women, who were supporting their partners emotionally and materially but sometimes getting little in return (Fishman, 1990).

### 3.2.2. Role Changes

Examination of Fishman's qualitative interview results revealed that relationships were sometimes compromised by the changes in roles that resulted from the men's absence. Women often became the major decision maker and head of the household, although some women tried to mitigate these changes by saving decisions for discussion during prison visits (Fishman, 1990). To counter changes in traditional gender roles, imprisoned men may seek unhealthy ways to assert their power, including entangling their partner in criminal activities by demanding that they bring in contraband or that they step into their former role in the drug trade. Men also may use dominance and threats to control women. Harassment and even violence have been reported during prison visits as men worry about losing their roles as husband and father in the family (Fishman, 1990; Nurse, 2002).

### 3.2.3. Psychological Changes

Harsh prison policies, rigid routines, deprivation of privacy and liberty, and a stressful environment all take their toll on men's psychological development. Inmates must adapt to unnatural living conditions, and these changes often conflict with the personality characteristics needed to sustain intimate relationships with partners and children. Because of the loss of autonomy, many men experience diminished capacity for decision making and greater dependence on outside sources. The prison environment also leads to hyper-vigilance as men worry about their safety, and this may result in interpersonal distrust and psychological distancing. The "prison mask" is a common syndrome that develops; the mask is the emotional flatness men take on when they suppress emotions and withdraw from healthy social interactions. To survive in an often brutal environment, prisoners may develop hyper- masculinity, which glorifies force and domination in relations with others. Finally, many prisoners are plagued by feelings of low self-worth and symptoms of posttraumatic stress disorder (Haney, 2001). All of these psychological changes, which may be necessary for survival in the prison environment, can impede intimate relationships.

> *The psychological changes necessary to survive in prison may impede the development of intimate relationships.*

## 3.3. ECONOMIC AND EMOTIONAL STRAINS ASSOCIATED WITH SINGLE PARENTING

Marital and partner bonds are also weakened by economic strain. The majority of families affected by incarceration are of low income (Mumola, 2000), and the men's earnings are important for making ends meet (even though some of those earnings may come from illegal sources). At the time of their arrest, 61% of fathers incarcerated in state prison were employed full-time and 12% were employed part-time or occasionally. However, 27% of incarcerated fathers in state prison report that the source of their income in the month prior to their arrest was illegal (Mumola, 2000). As noted earlier, 54% of fathers in state prison reported providing the primary financial support for their children prior to incarceration (Glaze & Maruschak, 2008).

The loss of direct income can create a significant burden on struggling families, especially when it is combined with the additional costs associated with arrest and imprisonment, including attorney fees, collect calls from prison, and the expenses of traveling to the prison and providing material goods for the inmate (Arditti, 2005). According to qualitative research conducted by Arditti, Lambert-Shute, and Joest (2003), the proportion of women working actually declined (from 89% to 64%) after their partners were incarcerated because of the need for childcare and other issues. Furthermore, many women had to go on public assistance as a result of their partner's incarceration.

For single mothers, the stress of financial hardship has been linked with psychological distress, negative parenting behaviors, and poor child outcomes (McLoyd, 1998). Single parenthood due to incarceration is a role taken on involuntarily, and anger and resentment about this new situation may weaken commitment to the imprisoned partner. Parenting also may become more challenging because many children whose parents are imprisoned show elevated rates of internalizing and externalizing problems (Jose-Kampfner, 1995; Murray & Farrington, 2005). Many women with an incarcerated partner see a reduction in available social support to cope with the stress associated with their partner's imprisonment as friends and family withdraw because of the stigma (Arditti et al., 2003). In addition, incarceration is marked as an "ambiguous loss" because the partner's absence is not publicly mourned or socially validated. This can lead to exacerbated grief and the phenomenon of being a "prison widow" (Arditti et al., 2003).

## 3.4. COMMUNITY-LEVEL EFFECTS

In neighborhoods with a high rate of arrest and release, the influence of incarceration can spread beyond the individual and the family and spill over into the community (Western & McLanahan, 2000). High incarceration rates can destabilize communities by increasing the number of families headed by low-income single mothers, stripping the community of much- needed fiscal resources, upsetting kin networks, and reducing informal social control, particularly over young adolescent males. Collective efficacy—a community's capacity to regulate socially acceptable behavior—is diminished by the disruption of incarceration (Sampson, Raudenbush, & Earls, 1997). The cycles of incarceration and release, combined with low collective efficacy, can result in even higher crime rates in the future, as subsequent generations are unable to prosper (Western, 2004). This fragmentation of community has been particularly harmful to African American communities who face disproportionately high rates of imprisonment exacerbated by racial inequities in drug laws (Clayton & Moore, 2003).

> *High incarceration rates can destabilize communities by increasing the number of families headed by low- income single mothers and reducing informal social control over adolescents.*

## 3.5. POSITIVE PERCEPTIONS OF PARTNER INCARCERATION FROM WOMEN

Although most women report incarceration as a negative event, some experience positive changes as a result of their partner's imprisonment. If a partner has been abusive toward the woman and/or children, his imprisonment is often a relief. Having a partner locked up also can be advantageous if criminal involvement was endangering the home life or if money was being drained from the family resources for drugs. Some women view this time away from their partner with hope, anticipating that the men will look upon prison as an opportunity for self-improvement and learn to appreciate their partner's devotion. Others use this time to conclude that they do not want to reunite. Women who have experienced domestic or family violence are the most likely to want to terminate the relationship (Fishman, 1990; Hairston & Oliver, 2006).

## 3.6. RESEARCH LIMITATIONS

Although the aforementioned literature provides descriptions of, and critical insights into, the types of challenges faced when couples are separated by imprisonment, this information was gathered largely through qualitative methods such as interviews and focus groups with small, nonrepresentative samples. These methods provide rich descriptions useful for informing public policy; however, more quantitative (and qualitative) research is needed using large, random samples of men in federal and state prisons and their partners in the community. These studies should use standardized measures to assess the degree to which prisoners (and their partners) differ from the general population in characteristics relevant to family life and well-being. Research involving couples from different racial/ethnic groups is important to inform culturally competent interventions and policies. Moreover, longitudinal research that follows individuals and their partners over time is critically needed. Prospective research will allow us to make causal inferences about the effects of the prison experience on the couple relationship. We are currently hindered from identifying any cause-and-effect relationships because of the correlational nature of the available data.

# Chapter 4

# THE EFFECTS OF PARENTAL INCARCERATION ON CHILDREN

This chapter discusses the adverse effects of parental incarceration on children and the types of stressors children experience because of their parent's arrest and imprisonment. The chapter concludes by identifying some protective factors that may promote resilience in children with an imprisoned parent.

> *Two percent of all children and almost seven percent of all African American children have a parent in prison.*

The proportion of children affected by parental incarceration has risen substantially in recent years. In 1986, 10 in every 1,000 children had a parent in prison or jail; by 1997, that rate had doubled to 20 per 1,000, or 2.0% of all American children (Eddy & Reid, 2003; Johnson, 2006). The number of children with an incarcerated father increased 77% from 1991 to 2004 (Glaze & Maruschak, 2008). In 1999, 6.7% of African American children and 2.4% of Latino children had an incarcerated parent, compared to 0.9% of white children. Compared to white children, African American children were seven and a half times more likely to experience the incarceration of a parent (Glaze & Maruschak, 2008).

As noted earlier, an estimated 2,473,300 children in the United States have a father incarcerated in prison or jail, and unpublished estimates by Mumola (2006) indicate that 7,476,500 children have a parent who is incarcerated or under correctional supervision.

# 4.1. NEGATIVE EFFECTS ON CHILD DEVELOPMENT

In addition to the great stress that incarceration places on the marital bond, it also negatively affects parenting efficacy and child development. Based on qualitative and cross-sectional quantitative studies, children of incarcerated parents appear more likely to experience a range of negative outcomes than children of similar socioeconomic backgrounds who do not have an incarcerated parent. Pathways for these effects remain unclear; however, a preliminary theoretical model articulated in Parke and Clarke-Stewart's (2001) meta-analysis proposes that incarceration weakens parent-child bonds, leading to insecure attachment, diminished cognitive abilities, and weak relationships with peers.

Because much existing research on the impact of parent imprisonment on child development is not specific to fathers, we draw on studies that investigated the influence of mother involvement in the criminal justice system as well. Children of incarcerated parents are more likely to experience internalizing disorders and to exhibit behavioral problems than their peers (Jose-Kampfner, 1995; Baunach, 1985). Based on a qualitative study of 30 children who had witnessed the arrest of their mothers, Jose-Kampfner (1995) posited that the high levels of anxiety and depression found among participants were associated with the experience of maternal incarceration and with trauma related to the arrest event itself. In her sample of 56 mothers incarcerated at women's prisons in Kentucky and Washington State and their children, Baunach (1985) found that 70% of the children exhibited symptoms of social and psychological disorders, such as aggression, hostility, and withdrawal. Preliminary research suggests that children with incarcerated parents may exhibit a range of academic problems, including poor grades, behavior problems, and school phobias at higher rates than children of nonincarcerated parents. Stanton (1980) compiled quantitative measures of childhood well-being for 166 children ages 6 and under whose mothers were incarcerated, and found that 70% exhibited poor academic performance.

Some studies of parental (father or mother) incarceration suggest that children whose parents spend time in prison are more likely to exhibit antisocial behavior, be involved with the criminal justice system as adolescents, and be incarcerated as adults compared with children who do not experience parental imprisonment. Murray and Farrington (2005) analyzed antisociality and delinquency data from the Cambridge Study in Delinquent Development, a longitudinal cohort of 411 London males and their parents. They compared boys who experienced parental incarceration any time from the age of 10 or younger with four control groups (boys who did not experience separation from their parents; boys who were separated from their parents by hospitalization or death; boys who were separated from their parents for other reasons, such as family discord; and boys whose parents were only incarcerated before their birth). They found that parental incarceration up through the age of 10 predicted severe antisocial-delinquent outcomes up to age 32 compared to the four control conditions, even after controlling for a number of other childhood risk factors. Murray, Janson, & Farrington's (2007) analysis of longitudinal data on 15,117 Swedish children collected as part of the Project Metropolitan study generated similar findings: children who experienced the incarceration of a parent from the age of 6 or younger were more than twice as likely to be convicted of a criminal offense between the ages of 19 and 30 compared with children who did not have a parent incarcerated during early childhood.

> *Children who experienced parental incarceration at age 6 or younger were more than twice as likely to be involved in the criminal justice system as young adults.*

It remains an empirical question whether the association between parental incarceration and negative child outcomes reflects a causal relationship. An analysis of data from an Australian cohort enrolled at birth and followed through age 14 found a significant association between paternal incarceration and negative child outcomes including substance use and internalizing and externalizing behavior (Kinner, Alati, Najman, & Williams, 2007). However, when socioeconomic status, maternal mental health and substance use, parenting style, and family adjustment were controlled, the associations became non-significant. Such findings highlight the uncertain status of the literature regarding whether parental incarceration itself leads to negative outcomes or is a marker for other background factors that erode child well-being (Phillips, Erkanli, Keeler, Costello, & Angold, 2006; Kinner et al., 2007; Hairston, 2008).

## 4.2. MECHANISMS OF RISK

Describing the mechanisms through which parental imprisonment affects child development is crucial for designing programs to ameliorate the negative effects. However, attempting to disentangle the influence of parental incarceration from the myriad of other risk factors to which many children of incarcerated fathers are exposed is a challenge that has been poorly met by the existing research literature. Many children of incarcerated parents live in impoverished households, are exposed to substance abuse, and have witnessed or been victims of family violence prior to the parent's arrest (Parke & Clark-Stewart, 2001). Rather than a discrete stressful event in children's lives, parental incarceration might be better conceived of as a chronic strain, interacting with a host of other risk factors (Johnson & Waldfogel, 2002).

> *Many children of incarcerated parents live in impoverished households, are exposed to substance abuse, and have witnessed or been victims of family violence prior to the parent's arrest.*

Parental incarceration is a process that unfolds over the course of many years and presents children with distinct challenges before, during, and after parental imprisonment (Hagan & Dinovitzer, 1999). At the time of arrest, children who reside with the arrested parent are frequently exposed to trauma (Jose-Kampfner, 1995). Those who witness the parent's arrest or criminal behavior often suffer nightmares and flashbacks (Johnston, 1991). The incarceration period itself presents children with a range of challenges, including separation issues, loss of family income, disruption in the home environment, and stigmatization. When the parent is released, a new set of stressors emerge (this topic is covered in more detail in Chapter 6). Below, we discuss primary stressors associated with parental incarceration.

### 4.2.1. Parental Separation

Separation is a significant challenge for children of incarcerated fathers, who are typically away from their parent much longer than children of incarcerated mothers (Parke & Clarke-Stewart, 2003). An average sentence for fathers in state prison is 12.5 years, approximately 5 years longer than the average sentence for mothers (Mumola, 2000).

> *One-third to one-half of incarcerated fathers never see their children during their imprisonment.*

Poehlmann's (2005) qualitative study of 94 incarcerated mothers indicated that more frequent contact during incarceration was associated with more positive parent-child relationships, particularly with older children. Contact, however, is limited when a parent is in prison. A recent study indicates that two-thirds of fathers had never received a visit from their child (Day et al., 2005). Lanier's (1991) random sample of 302 men incarcerated in a maximum-security prison in New York found that 30% of fathers participated in family reunion visits (24-hour "trailer visits") with their children, 43% participated in family picnic days with their children, and 67% received conventional visits from their children. Of those who received visits from their children, 37% reported that such visits occurred less than once a month. A majority of fathers reported regular "distal" interactions with their children: 64% reported phoning their children at least once a month, including 45% who phoned their children at least once a week; 73% reported sending mail to their children at least once a month; and 56% reported receiving mail from their children at least once a month. Both proximal and distal father-child interactions during incarceration were positively correlated with a father's residence with his children prior to incarceration and his expectations of residing with them after release (Lanier, 1991).

Based on national data from the 2004 Survey of Inmates, Glaze and Maruschak (2008) reported that 30% of fathers incarcerated in state prisons had some form of weekly contact with their children, and another 23% had some form of contact at least monthly. Seventeen percent of fathers reported contact less than once a month, and 22% had no contact with their children during the current incarceration. Mail was the most common form of contact fathers experienced, with 69% reporting any mail contact with a child during their incarceration. Fifty-three percent reported having any phone contact with a child during their incarceration, and 41% reported having any personal visit with a child (Glaze & Maruschak, 2008). Hairston, Rollin, and Jo's analysis of the 1997 Survey of Inmates data found that incarcerated fathers were less likely than incarcerated mothers to maintain contact with their children while in prison (2004). African American parents were somewhat more likely than white or Hispanic parents to report visitation or phone contact with their children during incarceration (Hairston, 2008).

Children may be prevented from contact with their parents because the custodial parents or other relatives do not want the children to know that one of their parents is incarcerated, do not want to expose them to the prison visitation environment, or cannot afford to maintain contact (Hairston, 2001). The distance between a prisoner's home and the facility at which he is incarcerated is a strong predictor of any in-person contact (Hairston, 2008). In addition, the quality of relationships between incarcerated parents and their children's caregivers appears to play a central role in determining frequency of parent-child contact (Poehlmann, 2005). For fathers who perpetrated domestic violence prior to incarceration, partners and caregivers may view the incarceration as a welcome reprieve for children who formerly witnessed or experienced violence in the home (Hairston and Oliver, 2006); in such cases, they are not likely to encourage maintenance of father- child contact during the incarceration.

### 4.2.2. Economic Hardship and Harsh Parenting

As discussed earlier, the loss of income brought about by imprisonment can present significant hardship to families. Although figures specific to the households of incarcerated fathers are not available, longitudinal data on divorced families indicate that family income falls by an average of 41% in the first year that one parent is absent (Page & Stevens, 2004). This magnitude of income loss can be particularly destabilizing in households that were struggling financially before an incarceration (Braman & Wood, 2003). Drawing on data from the Great Smoky Mountain study, a prospective cohort study of 1,400 children in North Carolina, (Phillips et al., 2006) found that parental incarceration was associated with family instability and economic strain, which are known risk factors for poor child outcomes. Other studies suggest that income loss may contribute to negative parenting and parenting stress, both of which are associated with poor socio-emotional outcomes among children (Braman & Wood, 2003; McLoyd, 1998).

### 4.2.3. Change in Caregivers

Another potential disruption in the child's life associated with parental incarceration is a change in the child's caregivers or the addition of a new member to the household (Johnson & Waldfogel, 2002; Nurse, 2004). For children who reside with a parent who becomes incarcerated, parental arrest can trigger placement in foster care, the introduction of new partners or family members into the household, and increased reliance on nonparent adults for care. Frequent changes in relationships appear to represent a common source of disruption in children's lives (Furstenburg, 1995; Nurse, 2004). Citing Whelan's (1993) finding that the presence of adults other than blood relatives in a child's home increases the chance of victimization, Johnston (2006) suggests that the relationship between parental incarceration and various negative child outcomes may be affected by changes in family structure and an associated increase in victimization experiences among children with an incarcerated parent as well as by incarceration itself.

Longitudinal data from the first three waves of the Fragile Families Study indicates that instability in the home environment, particularly changes in a mother's romantic relationships when a child is young, can lead to increased child behavioral problems. Following a sample of 2,111 children for 3 years, Osborne and McLanahan (2007) found that each change in a mother's romantic partnership was associated with an increase in children's anxiety, depression, and aggression. Furthermore, the influence of mother's relationship changes was largely mediated by maternal stress and negative parenting practices.

Out-of-home placement has been suggested as another contributor to the negative effect of incarceration on children's well-being. A study of 258 adolescents receiving mental health services found that out-of-home placement appeared to exacerbate the effect of incarceration on adolescents' emotional and behavioral problems (Phillips, Burns, Wagner, Kramer, & Robbins, 2002). The likelihood of placement with a nonparent increases with the presence of other psychosocial risk factors in the child's life, including low paternal or maternal educational attainment, public benefit receipt, and paternal or maternal history of abuse (Johnson & Waldfogel, 2002).

### 4.2.4. Stigma and Social Isolation

Initial qualitative findings from a 3-year ethnographic study of families of male prisoners in Washington, DC, suggest that children are also affected by social stigma during a parent's incarceration (Braman & Wood, 2003). Other qualitative work indicates that children of incarcerated parents may not be privy to the social support and sympathy otherwise afforded families experiencing the involuntary loss or absence of a family member (Arditti, 2005; Hagan & Dinovitzer, 1999). Children may be exposed to criticism of themselves or their mothers regarding their involvement or lack of involvement with their incarcerated father (Braman & Wood, 2003). Finally, children who maintain in-person contact with their fathers during incarceration may undergo potentially stigmatizing experiences in the correctional environment as part of the visitation routine (Arditti, 2005; Hairston, 2001).

---

*Because of stigma, children with fathers in prison are frequently denied the social support and sympathy provided to children experiencing other types of parental separation or loss such as divorce or death.*

## 4.3. PROTECTIVE FACTORS

Children differ in how they respond to parental incarceration. Factors such as positive relationships with other caregivers can protect children from negative outcomes (Parke & Clarke- Stewart, 2001). For example, a high-quality relationship with the imprisoned parent prior to the incarceration has been proposed as an important protective factor. The quality of a child's relationships with the remaining parent, extended family, and nonfamily adults also appears to predict better adjustment. Researchers have begun to suggest that the quality and frequency of contact with the incarcerated parent (if positive) can moderate negative child outcomes (Johnson, 2006; Arditti, 2005; Parke & Clarke-Stewart, 2001). These findings highlight protective factors which may be bolstered to support child-well being during parental imprisonment.

## 4.4. RESEARCH LIMITATIONS

An empirical understanding of the effect of paternal incarceration on children is beginning to emerge, particularly in the wake of several major longitudinal analyses of child outcomes in cohorts that included children of incarcerated parents (Murray & Farrington, 2005; Phillips et al., 2006; Kinner et al., 2007; Murray et al., 2007). Several serious limitations persist in the literature. Studies that aim to measure the effect of parental incarceration often do not distinguish between the experiences of children with incarcerated mothers and those with incarcerated fathers, even though researchers acknowledge that these experiences are likely quite different (Parke & Clarke-Stewart, 2003). More research is needed to distinguish the unique stressors and outcomes related to having a mother versus father incarcerated as well as the developmental implications of the timing of their imprisonment. Many studies of the children of prisoners have relied on data collected via surveys of the incarcerated parents (Johnston, 1995). Therefore, data on psychosocial outcomes in this population are based on secondhand reports rather than on direct administration of assessment tools to children. Future research should incorporate direct child assessments and observational studies of parent-child interaction. Most studies of the effects of parental incarceration have employed cross- sectional rather than longitudinal designs, have examined small and nonrepresentative samples, and rarely have been grounded in principles of child developmental or other theoretical perspectives (Parke & Clarke-Stewart, 2003). Of utmost importance is the need to conduct longitudinal, prospective studies that follow children through the various stages of their parents' involvement with the criminal justice system (arrest, sentencing, imprisonment, release) to assess changes in wellbeing over time and identify malleable risk and protective factors for future intervention. The limitations addressed here make it difficult to draw firm conclusions regarding differential outcomes for these children and even more challenging to determine causal pathways (Hagan & Dinovitzer, 1999).

*Chapter 5*

# REENTRY AND THE MARITAL/PARTNER RELATIONSHIP

With some exceptions, most men who are imprisoned return home. Reentry is the dynamic process of exiting prison and returning to a free society (Visher & Travis, 2003). Although this can be an exciting time for some families, it can be a fearful time for others (particularly those whose partners have a history of domestic violence). There are a number of challenges that men and women need to anticipate as men attempt to resume their roles as husbands/partners and fathers. The reentry experience for each inmate is shaped by his pre-incarceration history (e.g., substance abuse, domestic violence history, job skills and experience); his prison experience (i.e., mental and physical health status); and his attitudes, beliefs, and personality traits (Travis, Solomon, & Waul, 2001). This chapter focuses on common obstacles to family well-being, including role renegotiation, negative emotions, relapse, interpersonal conflict, and the threat of domestic violence.

## 5.1. THE IMPORTANCE OF FAMILY

Inmates frequently look first to their families to meet their immediate needs for money, housing, and emotional support (Fishman, 1990; Visher & Travis, 2003). The majority of prisoners being released report feeling close to their family, and 70% of the men in the Ohio Returning Home Study expected to live with their family upon release from prison (however, in this study the definition of family was not restricted to partners and children) (Visher, Baer, & Naser, 2006). Research suggests that married men who reside with their wives and children upon release have a more successful transition (Visher & Travis, 2003). Although families play a substantial role in the reentry process, the criminal justice system does little to prepare families for their reunion (Fishman, 1990).

> *Married men who reside with their wives and children upon release from prison have a more successful transition.*

## 5.2. REESTABLISHING ROLES

Very little research is available to reliably document the process of reintegrating into the marital/partner relationship at reentry. What we do know about this process comes from small qualitative studies of men who were imprisoned and released and their partners (Fishman, 1990; Hairston & Oliver, 2006). Thematic summaries from these qualitative interviews and focus groups suggest that reintegration often starts with a "honeymoon period," where the couple gets reacquainted.

Many women feel optimistic that their partner will fulfill the promises he made while in prison with regards to stopping his criminal behavior. However, numerous conflicts may arise as the couple attempts to reorganize their lives and reestablish their roles within both the relationship and the household (Fishman, 1990).

> *Recreating a sustainable family process that acknowledges the inevitable changes that take place during the period of imprisonment is one of the most challenging tasks that prisoners and their partners face upon release.*

One issue identified in the available research involves power struggles and renegotiation of roles. Ex-inmates who have been forced into dependency during their imprisonment may seek to assert their own power and control within their family upon return. However, women who gained independence and self-sufficiency during the time on their own may desire more egalitarian roles and struggle with their partner for control (Travis, McBride, & Solomon, 2005). On the other hand, men and women who desire traditional roles in their partnership may feel thwarted if the man has difficulties finding employment and establishing himself as the financial breadwinner (Fishman, 1990). Recreating a sustainable family process that acknowledges the inevitable changes that take place during the period of imprisonment is one of the most challenging tasks that prisoners and their partners face upon release.

## 5.3. DEALING WITH RESENTMENT AND NEGATIVE EMOTIONS

As couples seek to recreate the routines of daily life, numerous powerful emotions may emerge. Researchers leading the Safe Return Study conducted focus groups in four urban areas with men who were incarcerated and released within 2 years, as well as their wives and girlfriends (Hairston & Oliver, 2006). They found that resentment, fear, disappointment, and anger over past hurts were commonly expressed by these men and women. For men who have been used to suppressing their emotions in prison, communicating intense feelings, especially if they are negative, was difficult (Haney, 2001). Lack of contact can weaken bonds and impede healthy patterns of communication (Travis et al., 2005). Thus, many couples could benefit from assistance at post-release in working through these emotional struggles.

## 5.4. RESUMPTION OF CRIMINAL ACTIVITY OR SUBSTANCE USE

Insight from qualitative studies suggests that in order to cope with the trauma of separation, much of couples' conversations in prison focused on how things will change for the better upon release. Men talked about their personal transformations and women responded with hope and commitment to the future (Fishman, 1990). Although many of these promises may be sincere, the strains of reentry and opportunities with old friends often draw men back into their past criminal life. For women, who have held on to their partner's promises, seeing him fall back on his old criminal patterns can be devastating (Hairston & Oliver, 2006). The odds of success after reentry are not very high: 68% of men are arrested within 3 years of their release, and 52% are back in prison for a new offense or a parole violation (Visher & Travis, 2003). In addition, one month after release, 25% of men report drug use or alcohol intoxication and this percentage increases to 35% one year post-release. Substance use resumption was related to numerous post- release problems including difficulties with family relationships (Visher & Courtney, 2007).

## 5.5. CONFLICT AND DOMESTIC VIOLENCE

Although many ex-offenders have a history of violence, little is known about reentry and domestic violence (Hairston & Oliver, 2006). Given the high rate of substance use, which has been consistently associated with domestic violence, it is likely that domestic violence will be an issue for a subsample of released men and their partners. African American women and those whose partners have a history of violence are at highest risk during reentry (Hairston & Oliver, 2006).

Reuniting partners often face many points of conflict including suspected infidelity, differences in how children should be raised, and the threat of new relationships women may have developed during their partner's absence (Fishman, 1990; Hairston & Oliver, 2006). Conflict—especially conflict that occurs in conjunction with alcohol or drug use—can easily escalate to violence. Perceptions of low self-efficacy in relationships have been linked to under- and un-employment which is common among released prisoners (Babcock, Waltz, Jacobson, & Gottman, 1993). Changes to men's sense of power and self esteem that occur during imprisonment also may elevate risk for violence against women. In a qualitative study focused on men returning home, some ex-inmates believed violence against women was justified in order to gain control in the relationship (Hairston & Oliver, 2006). Violence against intimate partners is both a tactic to suppress woman's voices and a way to vent frustration (Jewkes 2002).

> *In a qualitative study focused on men returning home, some ex-inmates believed violence against women was justified.*

Intense treatment is needed for men with histories of family violence, and reunion with families should be treated with caution if women and children face any risk of emotional, physical, or sexual abuse. Not all batterers can and should be reunited with their partners; thus, family strengthening programs should include screening for domestic violence and safety planning (Bauer et al., 2007).

The goal of family strengthening efforts with this population must not be reunification at all costs, but the provision of interventions in situations where there is a reasonable likelihood of benefits.

Batterer interventions generally emphasize cognitive behavioral techniques and address power and control issues. Marital education approaches that emphasize skill development such as anger management, conflict resolution, negotiation, problem solving, and empathy may not be sufficient for this population. Batterer interventions based within a cognitive-behavioral paradigm target irrational "self-talk" that fuels abusive incidents. Negative/aggressive thoughts are identified and linked to feelings and behaviors. The batterer learns to preempt the escalation of negative thoughts using cognitive reframing and relaxation. Interventions grounded in feminist theory (Johnson, 1995) address the influence of the traditional patriarchal family structure, social constructions of masculinity and femininity, and asymmetry in male and female power (Johnson, 1995). From this perspective, men's violence is perceived as being rooted in a need to achieve power and control (Jewkes, 2002; Tilley & Brackley, 2005). Several batterer interventions utilize the "Power and Control Wheel," which illustrates how male power is demonstrated through control tactics such as minimizing, blaming, intimidation, emotional abuse, isolation, and economic threats. These abusive strategies are countered by teaching critical thinking skills, confrontational group processes, accountability-focused group therapy, and empathy and moral development (Healey, Smith, & O'Sullivan, 1998). However, the efficacy of batterer interventions has been shown to be modest at best (Babcock & LaTaillade, 2000).

More research is needed to increase understanding of how to reduce the risks of domestic violence using skill-building cognitive-behavioral techniques, and power/control paradigms within the continuum of services provided to incarcerated men (Bauer et al., 2007). The availability of effective domestic violence prevention programming is crucial to providing a safe context for any family strengthening approaches undertaken with this population.

## 5.6. RESEARCH LIMITATIONS

Further empirical research is needed to understand how reentry affects the partner relationship and vice versa. Although quite informative, the limited research on this topic is predominantly qualitative and based on small, nonrepresentative samples. Although some quantitative research has focused on the protective role of family on the ex-offender, research has neglected to examine how the released offender's attempts to reintegrate affect his partner, children, and family system. It is especially important to determine how and when conflict escalates to violence and what interventions and system changes are needed to protect women and children. Research that examines constructs known to affect marital/partner resilience such as conflict resolution, anger management, power/control, and social support need to be examined using validated scales to compare patterns across families with and without an ex-offender. Furthermore, longitudinal research is needed to examine how relationships change over time in order to identify key transitional points and mechanisms for intervention.

*Chapter 6*

# REENTRY AND PARENTING

Given the percentage of incarcerated men who are fathers, it is important to examine what happens to father-child relationships after reentry. Further, resumption of fathering activities could help to facilitate criminal desistance among released fathers. In a qualitative study of 200 low-income, noncustodial fathers, Edin et al (2001) found that participants who began to assume an active fathering role with one or more of their children also began gravitating toward employment in the formal economy and away from illegal activity. Research indicates that fathers' experiences in reestablishing their relationships with their children after release from prison vary widely and may depend on a number of barriers and facilitators, each of which is discussed in this chapter.

## 6.1. Barrier to Reforming the Parent-Child Bond

### *6.1.1. Co-Residence*

Structural issues such as housing, child support, and child welfare may place limits on fathers' abilities to reestablish their relationships with their children. One of the major changes to father-child relationships is co-residence: In one study of 32 fathers on parole, about half of the fathers reported having lived with at least one of their minor children prior to incarceration, but less than 20% reported living with their children after release (Bahr, Armstrong, Gibbs, Harris, & Fisher, 2005). In another study of 294 men in Cleveland, Ohio, 57% of men who were fathers of minor children lived with at least one of their children before incarceration, while only 35% lived with any of their children 1 year after reentry (Visher & Courtney, 2007). A lack of co-residence may be related to (1) the quality of the relationship that the father has with the children's primary caregiver (usually the mother); (2) rules forbidding former convicts to live in public or subsidized housing or in homes approved for relative foster care (Hairston, 2001; Festen, Waul, Solomon, & Travis, 2002; Jeffries, Menghraj, & Hairston, 2001); and (3) the possibility that other family members in the home are involved in substance use or criminal activity (Naser & Farrell, 2004; Visher & Travis, 2003), thereby endangering the father's ability to comply with parole requirements.

### 6.1.2. Interference from Mothers and Other Family Members

A second type of barrier to reestablishing the father-child relationship at release involves interference from the child's mother or other family members. In a study of 258 paroled fathers, 23% of respondents cited their relationships with their children's mothers as a primary determinant of their relationships with their children. Qualitative research with a subset of 20 fathers indicated that mothers controlled and regulated fathers' access to the children, and fathers tended to view their relationships with their children and the children's mothers as being intertwined (Nurse, 2004). If interparental relationships are strained, fathers often have little or no contact with their children while they are in prison and have difficulty reestablishing their relationships with their children after release (Festen et al., 2002; Hairston, 2001; Nurse, 2004). Mothers often enlist the assistance of their extended family in caring for their children while the father is in prison. These family members may have negative perceptions of the father and may disapprove of his involvement with the children. As a result, qualitative interviews with fathers suggest that fathers' relationships with mothers' family members also dictate whether fathers are able to see and spend time with their children after they are released (Nurse, 2004).

> *Fathers cite their relationships with their children's mothers as a primary determinant of their relationships with their children.*

### 6.1.3. New Father Figures

Related to this issue is the fact that other adult men may begin to serve as "father figures" in a child's life during a father's incarceration. In many cases, this person is the mother's boyfriend but may be an uncle, grandfather, or other male relative (Nurse, 2004). Qualitative interviews with incarcerated fathers revealed that they are often jealous of other men in their children's lives. This emotional challenge can cause tension with the children's mother and sometimes leads fathers to relinquish their attempts to be involved in their children's lives in order to avoid conflict (Palm, 2001; Nurse, 2004).

Nurse (2004) found that fathers reported more frequent contact with their children (at least several times per week on average) after release when the children's mother was single than when the mother was in a new intimate relationship (a few times a month on average) (Nurse, 2004).

### 6.1.4. Quality of Relationship During Incarceration

One of the most important predictors of father-child relationships upon reentry is the quality of these relationships while fathers are incarcerated (Festen et al., 2002). Many studies of incarcerated fathers (e.g., Hairston, 2001) have documented the dearth of contact that they have with their children while they are in prison. The multitude of barriers to visitation and contact make maintaining father-child relationships difficult. Descriptive studies of prison policies suggest that fathers are usually unable to have unsupervised conversations with their children and many times are not able to have physical contact with them (Bauer et al., 2007; Carlson & Cervera, 1992; Hairston, 1998). Nonetheless, there is some indication that fathers who have more contact with their children while incarcerated may be more successful in rebuilding their relationships with their children upon reentry (Hairston & Oliver, 2006; Festen et al., 2002). Researchers theorize that maintaining parenting roles during incarceration helps fathers transition back into such roles upon release (Adalist-Estrin, 1994).

### 6.1.5. Unrealistic Expectations

Research with prisoners awaiting release has found that fathers tend to have unrealistic expectations of their relationships with their children (Day et al., 2005; Schmitzer, 1999). A survey of 51 incarcerated fathers found that although more than half felt that they had close relationships with their children, 41% indicated that they never or rarely discussed their child's life with their partner and almost two-thirds reported never having received a visit from their child (Day et al., 2005). Additionally, a pilot study of 324 reentering prisoners in the Maryland Returning Home study revealed that fathers' expectations for renewing relationships with their children were met or exceeded after release: Whereas 79% of respondents thought before release that it would be "pretty easy" or "very easy" to renew relationships with their children, 94% of respondents indicated after release that this had been the case. In contrast, although more than two-thirds of respondents expected to see their children daily, just over half actually did have daily contact with their children 4 to 6 months after release (Naser & Farrell, 2004). Qualitative data suggest that incarcerated fathers may idealize their relationships with their children and fantasize about activities they will do together when they are released (Adalist-Estrin, 1994; Nurse, 2004). The realities faced once fathers are released can be difficult to cope with.

### 6.1.6. Prisonization

A final set of barriers to parenting upon reentry, which has been the most widely addressed in prison parenting and family- based programs, involves the experiences of fathers in prison. The prison environment is highly structured and controlled, and gives fathers little autonomy or need to make decisions for themselves. Displays of aggression and dominance are sometimes essential to safety and success in prison, and fathers learn to withdraw socially and become distrusting and psychologically remote. These characteristics run counter to the qualities that are likely to support close relationships between fathers and their children (Festen et al., 2002; Hairston, 2001; Haney, 2001). The psychological changes that take place when fathers are incarcerated therefore may impede their ability to connect and reestablish intimacy with their children, to help organize their children's environment, and to make authoritative decisions for their children (Festen et al., 2002; Haney, 2001).

## 6.2. CHILD SUPPORT PAYMENTS

Child support demands present major difficulties to incarcerated and reentering fathers. A study of inmates in Massachusetts found that 22% of inmates under Department of Correction (DOC) jurisdiction were part of the child support caseload; a Colorado study found that 26% of inmates in state prison facilities and 28% of parolees were involved with the child support system. (Griswold & Pearson, 2003). Incarcerated fathers often enter prison with child support debt. Child support obligations continue when fathers become incarcerated, but it is usually impossible for inmates to meet their child support obligations. Child support order amounts are based on the earnings of parents at the time of the order, and most inmates earn little or no income. For instance, inmates in Massachusetts may earn as little as $1 per day, and inmates in Colorado earn between 25¢ and $2.50 per day (Griswold & Pearson, 2003). These factors combine to leave fathers with large amounts of child support debt owed upon release from prison. Analyses of child support profiles in Massachusetts indicated that released prisoners owe an average of over $16,000 in child support debt, including both pre- and during-prison nonpayments; increases in debt during incarceration averaged over $5,000 (Griswold & Pearson, 2003). One of the parolees in a Utah study accrued $30,000 in back support debt (Bahr et al., 2005). Child support debt is compounded by other debts commonly imposed upon incarcerated fathers, including punitive fines, restitution payments, and judicial system cost- recovery assessments (Levingston & Turetsky, 2007).

> *Men released from prison in Massachusetts owe an average of $16,000 in child support debt.*

As child support debt continues to accumulate upon release from prison, limited skills, along with a record of incarceration, can make finding employment difficult (Bahr et al., 2005; Festen et al., 2002; Hairston, 2001). Child support demands may lead to recidivism if fathers are unable to find legal sources of income (Festen et al., 2002; Griswold & Pearson, 2003; Hairston, 2001). At the same time, nonpayment of child support may lead to re-arrest and reincarceration (Festen et al., 2002; Hairston, 2001; Travis et al., 2003). Difficulties paying child support can also impede father-child relationships by causing tension between fathers and their children's caregivers, to whom they owe the money (Hairston, 2001; Travis et al., 2003), or by presenting legal barriers to fathers' contact with their children (Brenner, 1999).

The problems encountered by incarcerated and reentering fathers regarding issues of child support have prompted some states to implement laws, policies, and programs that help to reduce incarcerated fathers' payment obligations or to increase fathers' abilities to pay, and have led researchers to call for better integration between corrections and child support enforcement systems (Griswold & Pearson, 2003, OCSE, 2006). Child support agencies have also been experimenting with special projects to address these issues (OCSE, 2006). In addition, Levingston & Turetsky (2007) propose identifying outstanding debt and financial obligations as part of the prison intake process; offering debt management and repayment assistance to fathers after release; and giving higher priority to payment of reasonable child support obligations to families than to obligations such as state judicial system cost recovery.

## 6.3. Involvement in the Child Welfare System

Another challenge to father-child relationships is that some children are placed into the child welfare system during the father's imprisonment. Although the proportion of children of incarcerated fathers in foster care is smaller than that of children of incarcerated mothers (approximately 2% compared to 10%), the number of children is actually larger because there are about ten times the number of incarcerated fathers. (Travis, McBride, & Solomon, 2003; Glaze and Maruschak, 2008). It is often hard for fathers to locate their children when they are in foster care, making it even more difficult for these fathers to reconnect with their children upon reentry (Hairston, 1998, 2001; Jeffries et al., 2001; Travis et al., 2003). In addition, case workers who attempt to contact nonresident fathers regarding their children's placements face numerous obstacles which are typically exacerbated by a father's current or recent incarceration (Malm, Murray & Geen, 2006). Incarcerated fathers are rarely involved in decisions regarding the placement of their children (Hairston, 1998, 2001). These issues have led researchers to call for policies that are more sensitive to the desires of fathers to be involved in such decisions and for further integration of corrections and child welfare systems (Malm, Murray & Geen, 2006; Hairston, 1998, 2001; Rossman, 2001). Conway & Hutson, (2007) suggest that child welfare agencies should provide supports for parent-child reunification when the parent of a child in foster care is incarcerated. Suggested support services include: case planning for economic stability, including services to help released parents of children in foster care obtain employment; services to strengthen parent-child relationships, such as parenting education and special visitation programs; and mental health and substance abuse treatment.

## 6.4. Risk of Child Abuse

Research has not documented the prevalence of child abuse among children of incarcerated fathers or the implications of incarceration and reentry for child abuse. Nonetheless, programs that aim to strengthen father-child relationships of incarcerated fathers tend to exclude fathers who are incarcerated because of crimes against children (Dunn & Arbuckle, 2002; Jeffries et al., 2001). Researchers acknowledge that it is sometimes not safe for fathers to reestablish relationships with their children upon release from prison because of prior involvement in family violence. More intensive clinical efforts are needed for this group of fathers if they are to reconnect with their children (Festen et al., 2002; Travis, Solomon, & Waul, 2001).

To ensure that children are protected, more attention to issues of child abuse and well-being is needed in planning for reentry of incarcerated fathers.

## 6.5. POSITIVE PARENTING RELATIONS AND CRIMINAL DESISTANCE

Fathers clearly face many challenges to reestablishing their relationships with their children upon release from prison. In turn, the quality of these relationships may affect their reentry success. Unfortunately, most studies that have found associations between family closeness and support and reduced criminal involvement have focused on the family network in general and on fathers' intimate partner relationships and relationships with their own parents in particular (e.g., Bahr et al., 2005; Bobbitt & Nelson, 2004; Visher & Courtney, 2007; Visher & Travis, 2003). Nonetheless, the study of returning prisoners in Cleveland found that fathers' attachment to children was negatively related to fathers' substance use one year after release; their attachment was not related to employment, re-arrest, or reincarceration (Visher & Courtney, 2007). This study also found that before release, 46% of fathers cited spending time with children as a factor that would be important to staying out of prison; after release, about 10% cited seeing their children as an inhibitor of returning to prison (Visher & Courtney, 2007).

> *Fathers who had contact with their children while in prison, and those who had better relationships with their children upon release, were less likely to return to prison.*

Qualitative interviews with 20 former prisoners who had since desisted from crime also support the importance of fathers' relationships with their children as a protective factor (Hughes, 1998). Bahr and colleagues' (2005) small study of parolees found that fathers who had contact with their children while in prison, and those who had better relationships with their children upon release, were less likely to return to prison. Additionally, a study of 302 incarcerated fathers found that those who have more positive perceptions of their relationships with their children tend to report better psychological wellbeing (Lanier, 1993). Fathers who had contact with their children while in prison, and those who had better relationships with their children upon release, were less likely to return to prison. These findings are consistent with social support and primary relationship frameworks, which suggest that social support from family members and involvement in important family roles limit deviant tendencies and promote mental health (Hairston, 1988; Jeffries et al., 2001; Visher & Travis, 2003).

## 6.6. RESEARCH LIMITATIONS

Much of the research examining the links between prisoner reentry and father-child relationships is based on qualitative interviews with small samples of fathers (for exceptions, see Bahr et al., 2005; Naser & Farrell, 2004; Visher & Courtney, 2007). Therefore, more rigorous investigations with representative samples of diverse offenders are needed to examine (1) processes through which the fathers reestablish relationships with their children; (2) how these may differ by family structure, culture, and father-child characteristics; and (3) what factors promote positive father-child involvement.

*Chapter 7*

# FAMILY STRENGTHENING PROGRAMS

## 7.1. MARRIAGE AND RELATIONSHIP EDUCATION PROGRAMS IN PRISON

Given the potential deleterious effects that imprisonment can have on spouse/partner and father-child involvement, research into preventive interventions is warranted. Interventions focused on marital education, parenting behaviors, and other life skills have strong potential to strengthen families; lessen family conflict, dissolution, and violence; and prevent child behavioral problems and recidivism. This chapter focuses on marital, parenting, and family interventions and the evidence of their effectiveness by modality.

> *Teaching incarcerated fathers and their partners relationship skills may help the reentry transition and reduce recidivism.*

### 7.1.1. Group Classes

The majority of prison marriage and relationship education programs are designed as a series of group classes. They usually involve both incarcerated men and their partners, although the value of programming for men alone may have merits as well (Kaslow, 1987). Couples generally meet with a facilitator, clinician, or chaplain at the prison, with meetings sometimes structured around visitation times (Bauer et al., 2007; Markman, Eason, & Grant, 2005). Relationship education programs focus on a variety of content areas, including

- communication,
- emotional understanding,
- problem solving,
- conflict resolution,
- affection and intimacy,
- managing complex family relationships,
- changing attitudes and behaviors, ▪ assertiveness,
- stress management, and
- building trust and commitment.

Facilitator instruction is combined with videos, worksheets and activities, and role plays; couples are given the opportunity to practice their newly learned skills and discuss issues of concern with the help of the facilitator (Accordino & Guerney, 1998).

Evaluations are beginning to demonstrate evidence for the efficacy of relationship education classes in group settings. For instance, an evaluation of the PREP Inside and Out Program found improvements from pre-test to post-test in negative couple interaction, communication skills, relationship satisfaction, and feelings of loneliness; ratings of couple relationship outcomes were high (Markman et al., 2005; this example relationship education program is described in more detail in the box below). Additionally, a quantitative and qualitative evaluation of the Relationship Enhancement program, a 2-day group program with prisoners and their wives that focuses on teaching nine relationship skills, suggested that the 90 participants from the program over the course of 3 years were very satisfied with the content and format of the program, its leaders, and its ability to help them improve their relationships (Accordino & Guerney, 1998). Program effects on relationship skills or marital outcomes were not assessed, however. Stronger and longer-term evaluations of marriage and relationship education initiatives currently underway have the potential to further inform the development of efficacious prison-based programs (Bauer et al., 2007).

> **Example Marriage and Relationship Education Program in Prisons**
>
> PREP Inside and Out (Markman et al., 2005; Bauer et al., 2007)
> The Prevention and Relationship Education Program (PREP) was developed to assist couples in developing strong and healthy marriages. The goal of the program is for couples to learn how to prevent or reduce negative patterns in their relationship and to enhance personal, emotional, and commitment safety. The Oklahoma Department of Corrections has designated PREP as an official program to implement in its state prisons. Prison chaplains are trained to provide voluntary classes to inmates and their partners who are interested in learning more about relationships. The original PREP has been adapted for use with a prison population, including examples that are relevant to the lives of inmates, adherence to prison rules, and a schedule that takes into account visitation times. The 2-hour classes take place once per week for 6 weeks. The program focuses on communication skills, commitment, negative affect management, respect, mate selection, aggression, and positive connections.
>
> A one-group pre- and post-test evaluation was conducted with 177 male prisoners, 162 of whom were in a relationship with a current partner and 40% of whom were currently married. The study found beneficial effects of participation in the program on negative couple interaction, communication skills, relationship satisfaction, and feelings of loneliness; ratings of couple relationship outcomes were high. A 30-day follow-up study indicated that benefits were maintained. Inmates are currently being trained to deliver PREP, and the program is required for all inmates and their fiancés prior to getting married within the Oklahoma prisons.

## 7.1.2. Couples Counseling

Similar to marital education in a group format, couples counseling workshops have been used in prisons to strengthen intimate partner relationships (Showalter & Jones, 1980). In these sessions with small groups of couples or one-on-one, discussion may focus on (1) changes experienced by each partner during incarceration, (2) communication skills, deciding to continue or terminate the relationship, effects of stress and tension, and (5) community resources and support (Showalter & Jones, 1980). Social workers may work with the couples and provide feedback on their progress (Showalter & Jones, 1980). Additional recommendations for topics to address through one-on-one couples counseling include inmates' and their partners' negative feelings and concerns surrounding the incarceration and separation, joint decision-making and problem-solving, issues related to co- parenting and the inmate's relationship with the children, and preparations for reentry (Carlson & Cervera, 1992; Kaslow, 1987). Individual and group counseling efforts for incarcerated fathers and their partners have not been empirically evaluated; therefore the efficacy of this approach is unknown.

### 7.1.3. Furlough Programs

Another prison-based program approach designed to enhance relationships between incarcerated fathers and their spouses is conjugal visit or furlough programs. These programs involve extended (overnight) visits between incarcerated men and their spouses (and sometimes children) in separate on-site facilities, or temporary releases of inmates to the community for the purposes of reentry preparation. These programs are typically limited to prisoners who have no disciplinary history within the prison, and programs focused on family visits generally include prisoners who are legally married. These selection requirements yield a selective sample of incarcerated fathers who are likely to have better family relationships. The effects of enhanced visiting or furlough programs are mixed. For instance, a comparison of male prisoners released from Massachusetts prisons in 1973 (N=966) and 1974 (N=911) indicated that those who had received furloughs were less likely to return to prison within 1 year than were those who had not, even after controlling for selection factors in granting furloughs (LeClair & Guarino-Ghezzi, 1991).

> *Male prisoners in Massachusetts who received furloughs were less likely to return to prison within one year after release compared with those who did not receive furloughs.*

Howser and MacDonald (1982) examined the effects of the Family Reunion Program in New York State, which was an on- site private family visiting program offered to inmates who were not eligible for the state's regular furlough programs. The objectives of the program were to strengthen inmates' family relationships and to facilitate their adjustment to the community after release. Accommodations in mobile homes were provided at the prisons, but families were required to provide their own transportation and meals. Evaluations of this program found high rates of living with family upon release (87%). Program participants also exhibited lower rates of return to Department custody (4%) than expected given the overall return rates of released prisoners in the Department (11%). In contrast, participation in the California Family Visiting Program, which allowed inmates to spend up to 2 days in private visits on the prison grounds with members of their immediate family, and the Temporary Release Program, which allowed inmates about to be paroled to make visits to their home communities in order to spend time with their families and prepare themselves for release, was not related to recidivism rates, but was related to fewer arrests and parole violations (28 and 29%, respectively, for participants in the two programs versus 43% for non-participants; Holt & Miller, 1972) Moreover, although a sample of 33 participants in the New York Family Reunion Program described above reported increased closeness with their wives and children, few differences between these participants and other prisoners who engaged in regular family visitation were documented in terms of coping, decision-making balance with their wives, or cohesion and adaptability (Carlson & Cervera, 1992).

### 7.1.4. Marriage and Family Strengthening Grants for Incarcerated Fathers and their Partners

On September 30, 2006, with funding provided by the Deficit Reduction Act of 2005, the Department of Health and Human Services' Administration for Children and Families (ACF), Office of Family Assistance (OFA) announced grant awards to 226 organizations to promote healthy marriage and responsible fatherhood. Thirteen of these awards were funded under the Responsible Fatherhood, Marriage and Family Strengthening Grants for Incarcerated and Re-entering Fathers and Their Partners (MFS-IP) priority area. MFS-IP grantees include government (state, local, and tribal) and private (community- and faith-based) organizations. With a funding level of up to $500,000 per year for five years, the programs implemented under the MFS-IP priority area are designed to promote and sustain healthy marriages and strengthen families affected by incarceration.

MFS-IP grants support the provision of services to promote or sustain healthy relationships for couples with children, where one of the parents is incarcerated or otherwise involved with the criminal justice system (e.g., recently released from incarceration or under parole or probation). In addition to marriage-strengthening activities, grantees may deliver services that improve parenting and promote economic stability. Grantees must develop partnerships involving the criminal justice system and diverse community sectors. The grant also requires that program participation be voluntary and that grantees collaborate with domestic violence experts in the development of their programs.

## 7.1.5. Research Limitations on Marriage and Relationship Education Programs

Recently published reviews of the marriage-strengthening literature concur that, including lack of control/comparison groups, short follow-up periods, and use of non-standardized measures. Evaluation results are particularly limited for programs targeting racial and ethnic minorities (Larson, 2004), couples with low education and income, and couples with ambiguous commitments who have children out of wedlock (Markman et al., 2005). As these types of couples are more likely to face father incarceration, further investigation into marriage and family strengthening efforts for these populations are needed. An important first step would be to identify and describe the proportion of prisons that offer marriage and relationship education as well as the incarcerated fathers who take advantage of these programs. Additionally, evaluations of the types of programs described above should include larger samples, equivalent comparison groups, and longer-term assessment of outcomes.

Given the seeming dearth of prison programs for couples, future efforts can draw from other intervention models with similar populations, such as Behavioral Couples Therapy for substance abusing parents (Fals-Stewart, Birchler, & Kelley, 2006). The PREP Inside and Out and Relationship Enhancement programs are good examples of universal relationship education programs that have been adapted for incarcerated parents; stronger evaluation methods utilizing random assignment and control groups are needed to provide further evidence of the efficacy of these programs. More efforts to tailor existing evidence-based approaches for use in prisons are needed. New and innovative approaches also may be necessary to deal with the complexity of issues faced by incarcerated men.

Evaluations underway within the MFS-IP demonstration grants will yield important information about marriage/partner interventions provided during incarceration and after release. The 13 grantees are required to assess the extent to which their programs achieved their stated objective. Evaluation efforts primarily focus on knowledge gained from curriculum- based program components (such as parenting and marriage education curricula) and any changes in relationship quality (including communication and conflict resolution) immediately following marriage/partner education classes and workshops.

## 7.2. PARENTING PROGRAMS IN PRISON

Research indicates that prison-based parenting programs are offered to a minority of fathers. Eleven percent of fathers in state prison report ever participating in parenting or childrearing classes (Glaze and Maruschak, 2008). A 1999 report on state initiatives to encourage responsible fatherhood documented that only 11 states were implementing prison- based educational programs for fathers as part of their initiatives (Bernard & Knitzer, 1999). A recent survey of 315 state prisons found that 90% of female-only prisons offered or contracted out parenting programs, while only 41% of male- only prisons and 55% of coed prisons did so (Hughes & Harrison-Thompson, 2002). In 93% of the cases, these programs were offered on a voluntary or first-come, first- served basis. A recent U.S. Department of Justice report using data from 54 Departments of Corrections (48 of which were state DOCs) stated that basic parenting classes were offered in at least one women's facility in 94% of DOCs and in at least one men's facility in 85% of DOCs. In contrast, parenting classes with children present were offered to women in 26% of DOCs and to men in 11% of DOCs. Programs that take place outside of the secure prison facilities were only offered to men by three DOCs (LIS, Inc., 2002). It is likely that discrepancies across surveys in the proportions of prisons found to offer parenting programs for fathers result from different methods of identifying samples and measuring services for parents. Nonetheless, as preliminary evidence accumulates for the efficacy of prison-based parenting programs, broader dissemination is needed, particularly for fathers.

---

*Only 11 percent of fathers in state prison report ever participating in a parenting class.*

---

### 7.2.1. Group Classes

Like marriage- and relationship-strengthening programs, parenting programs most often take the form of group classes delivered in prisons (Brenner, 1999; Hughes & Harrison- Thompson, 2002; Jeffries et al., 2001). Such programs cover a variety of content, including

- child development,
- communication with children and other family members,
- discipline techniques,
- anger management,
- the importance of fathers' involvement,
- co-parenting relationships,
- rebuilding trust, and
- values and spirituality.

Facilitator instruction is combined with videos, worksheets, group discussion, activities such as stories and games, and role playing. In addition, a few educational programs invite men to read a children's book on audiotape and send it to their children along with a personal message (Palm, 2001; LIS, Inc., 2002). Other programs combine structured classes with self-guided study material and special events and projects (Hairston & Lockett, 1987). Occasionally, programs invite the children's mothers to participate in one or more classes (Jeffries et al., 2001) or have parallel groups in the community for custodial parents (Adalist-Estrin, 1994).

Few studies to date have examined the effectiveness of these types of interventions to improve parenting relationships among incarcerated fathers and their children. Most programs have asked for participants' feedback at the end of the sessions. Fathers generally state that programs have (1) helped them learn new parenting skills and information about their children, (2) strengthened their relationships with their children and led to increased contact with their children, and (3) taught them the importance of their roles as fathers (Dunn & Arbuckle, 2002; Hairston & Lockett, 1987; LaRosa & Rank, 2001; Palm, 2001; Skarupski et al., 2003).

Some studies employing nonexperimental pre- and post-test designs have suggested the possible effectiveness of prison- based education programs to improve parenting knowledge, attitudes, and behaviors (Cornille et al., 2005; Hairston & Lockett, 1987; LaRosa & Rank, 2001; LIS, Inc., 2002). For example, the DADS Family Project offered face-to-face and videoconference sessions designed to build self-efficacy and develop parenting skills among incarcerated men. Participants in both the videoconference and in-person sessions showed a significant increase in self-efficacy for avoiding harsh parenting; those in the videoconference group also showed statistically significant increases in self-efficacy for permitting self- expression and not using physical punishment (Cornille et al., 2005).

Additionally, a few experimental designs with randomly assigned treatment and control groups and pre- and post-test surveys have been used. Assessing the effects of a ten-week group fatherhood class offered by the Fairfax County Department of Community Corrections, Robbers (2005) found that fathers who received the class experienced increased frequency of child contact, increased fatherhood knowledge and improved attitudes toward fatherhood compared with fathers who did not receive the class. Bayse, Allgood, and Van Wyk's (1991) evaluation found improved family functioning and decreased self-focus among 54 incarcerated men who participated in a four-session family life education program that involved lectures, discussion, and homework assignments. The evaluation of

Oklahoma's Parental Training for Incarcerated Fathers program assigned 30 male inmates to either a control group or to a treatment group that received a 6-week parenting education and behavior management training intervention. Findings indicated improved parenting-related attitudes among participants in the fathers program but no significant impact on self-esteem or on children's self-perceptions (Harrison, 1997). An evaluation of a popular prison-based parenting program for fathers found positive effects of the intervention on father-child contact but not on a variety of parenting attitudes and parent- child relationship indices (Skarupski et al., 2003; this example parenting program is described in more detail in the box below).

---

**Example Parenting Education Program in Prisons Long Distance Dads** (Skarupski Et Al., 2003)

The Long Distance Dads (LDD) program is a character-based educational and support program developed by the Pennsylvania Department of Corrections at the State Correctional Institution at Albion. The LDD program is designed to assist incarcerated men in developing skills to become more involved and supportive fathers. Trained inmate peer leaders facilitate the program in 12 weekly group sessions. The sessions are structured in a small group format (8 to 10 inmates per group) with at least one peer leader per group. The focus of the LDD program is on (1) promoting responsible fatherhood and holistic parenting; (2) empowering fathers to assume emotional, moral, spiritual, psychological, and financial responsibility for their children, both during and upon release from incarceration; (3) accentuating the psycho-social development of both father and child;(4) meeting the challenges of being an incarcerated father; and (5) increasing the knowledge base concerning fatherhood.

A time series, matched control design was used to measure baseline and post-program changes in knowledge, attitudes, skills, and behaviors among LDD participants. The study had four components: survey of inmates, caregiver telephone interviews, face-to-face inmate interviews, and institutional data collection. At post-test, the men who participated in LDD scored higher/better than men who did not participate in the fatherhood program in two areas: (1) the average number of letters father reported sending home to children and (2) the total contact with child per year on average. This difference, however, was not corroborated by the caregiver interviews.

While quantitative analyses indicated that the LDD program may not be reaching its potential, the qualitative results suggest that this fathering program has some promise. The program is quite popular with the inmates as evidenced by an extensive waiting list, and the inmates appear to be satisfied with the program and hold it in high regard. In addition, based on the random sample of inmates interviewed, approximately half gained knowledge and skills from the program and nearly 70% learned about dealing with anger. Thus, there is a solid framework of inmate support for the program. For more information, see Skarupski et al., 2003.

Additionally, more rigorous efforts are underway. For instance, an adapted version of the Strengthening Families Program, an evidence-based program shown to prevent adolescent risk behavior in high-risk families, is being implemented with inmates and their children in Maryland and is being evaluated for possible impacts on parenting skills, substance use, and arrest outcomes (Jeffries et al., 2001). An experimental evaluation of a parent training program, in which one group receives a parent training manual and another group receives the manual plus classroom training, involves interviews at baseline and 12-month follow-up with inmates, their oldest children aged 3 to 10 years, and the children's primary caregivers (Eddy et al., 2001). Several other parenting programs for incarcerated fathers are also being evaluated, and the results of these efforts will help to improve services in the future.

### 7.2.2. Group Therapy

Group therapy or counseling sessions are another type of program that has been offered to incarcerated fathers (Jeffries et al., 2001; Magaletta & Herbst, 2001). The goal of these programs is often to empower fathers to improve their parenting attitudes and behaviors to prevent violence and enhance relationships (Jeffries et al., 2001). The Helping Offenders Pursue Excellence (HOPE) for Life program pairs fathers with juvenile offenders, so each can understand the other's perspective, and involves the fathers' family members in therapy when possible (Magaletta & Herbst, 2001). Clinicians suggest that group therapy sessions provide a solution to the problem of social alienation; allow fathers to access one another as resources; and help fathers learn that being available to their children while in prison, even if they cannot do things for them, is positive fathering (Magaletta & Herbst, 2001). Unfortunately, research has not been conducted to evaluate the effects of group therapy approaches with incarcerated fathers on parent-child relationships and post- release success.

### 7.2.3. *Programs with Children*

Some prison parenting programs involve children. These programs usually incorporate enhanced visitation and/or parent-child play activities, which may or may not be supervised by program staff (Adalist-Estrin, 1994; Brenner, 1999; Dunn & Arbuckle, 2002; Hughes & Harrison-Thompson, 2002; Jeffries et al., 2001; Landreth & Lobaugh, 1998). Such programs tend to be limited to fathers who have not committed serious institutional violations, are not sex offenders, and are not using substances (Dunn & Arbuckle, 2002). The goal of these programs is to improve the quality of father-child relationships by improving the atmosphere in which fathers and children interact. For instance, allowing fathers and children to have physical contact and play together in a child-friendly area is theorized to help them become more comfortable interacting (Dunn & Arbuckle, 2002). Also allowing fathers to have more private time interacting with their children may enable them to talk about sensitive issues and enhance their feelings of parental efficacy (Dunn & Arbuckle, 2002). A conceptual model of filial therapy suggests that supporting interactive child- centered play between fathers and children teaches fathers how to convey acceptance, empathy, and can help promote positive emotional bonds (Landreth & Lobaugh, 1998).

Preliminary evidence supports these approaches. For instance, fathers in the Living Interactive Family Education (LIFE) program, an enhanced visitation program in which fathers and children engage monthly in curricular and recreational activities together, reported in qualitative interviews and focus groups that the atmosphere of the program and the constructive parent-child interaction it promoted were important to program impacts. Participants also perceived improvement in their relationships and communication with their children, increased family unity, and development of life skills and improved behavior in their children (Dunn & Arbuckle, 2002). However, quantitative data measuring changes in such outcomes were not collected. In contrast, Landreth and Lobaugh (1998) examined the effects of a 10-week filial therapy program with incarcerated fathers in Texas using a randomized waitlist control design. Their evaluation with 32 fathers found significant differences between experimental and control participants with respect to their acceptance of the children, parenting stress, and children's problem behaviors at post-test. Given that parenting programs in male-only prisons are less likely to offer enhanced child visitation than are programs in female-only prisons (Hughes & Harrison-Thompson, 2002), it will be important for future research to build on these evaluations in order to create support for the use of such services with fathers.

> *Evaluation results suggest that parenting classes can increase parental acceptance of children and reduce parenting stress and children's acting out behavior.*

Some family strengthening efforts focus solely on children of incarcerated parents. For instance, the Mentoring Children of Prisoners program was established by the U.S. Department of Health and Human Services in 2003 to make competitive grants to applicants serving urban, suburban, rural, or tribal populations with substantial numbers of children of incarcerated parents and to support the establishment and operation of mentoring programs. Projects funded under this program link children with mentors, incorporate the elements of Positive Youth Development, and partner with private business, nonprofit, community–based, state, and local entities to support and enhance mentoring programs. This may include connecting children and families to additional support services. Funding supports the recruitment, screening, and training of mentors; the identification of children; the matching of children with suitable adult mentors; and the support and monitoring of the mentoring relationship.

In addition to the 13 MFS-IP grants mentioned previously, the Office of Family Assistance within the Administration for Children and Families/HHS has funded additional programs that target incarcerated fathers and their children under the Healthy Marriage and Responsible Fatherhood Promotion provisions of the Deficit Reduction Act of 2005. These programs enable fathers to improve their relationships and reconnect with their children, helping fathers overcome obstacles and barriers that often prevent them from being the most effective and nurturing parents possible.

### 7.2.4. Other Efforts to Address Parenting

Other types of evidence-based practices used with children and families could be tailored to children of incarcerated fathers to reduce the deleterious effects of father imprisonment (Murray & Farrington, 2006). Recently, a review of fatherhood initiatives identified 35 effective or promising programs utilizing various strategies with diverse populations, yet only two of these programs focused on incarcerated fathers (Bronte-Tinkew, Carrano, Allen, Bowie, Mbawa, & Mathews, 2007). Nonetheless, several of the evidence-based program approaches included in the review and the characteristics that underlie their effectiveness might be effective with incarcerated fathers. More research is needed to adapt and disseminate these approaches within the criminal justice system.

Other types of interventions drawn from child welfare, physical and mental health, and criminal justice systems may also help alleviate negative outcomes in families affected by incarceration. Examples include communication about parental absence, stable care placement, contact with the imprisoned parent, and therapeutic services. Nurse home visiting, parent management training, multisystemic therapy, and multidimensional treatment foster care are all community- based parenting programs are other promising approaches.

Financial assistance, cost subsidies, and prisoner employment may help to reduce economic strain among incarcerated fathers and their families. Finally, criminal justice-based approaches such as introducing anonymity of offenders, implementing restorative justice approaches, and using strengths-based sentencing can help reduce the stigma associated with incarceration that can be harmful to children and families. Future research should address the efficacy of these services with incarcerated families and examine how organizational climates and integrated service delivery strategies can facilitate these approaches.

## 7.3. REHABILITATION PROGRAMS

Because healthy marriages and positive parenting can be adversely affected by problems such as unemployment and substance abuse, programs that impact these domains could conceivably produce benefits to the family. Prison-based educational programs have been shown to increase annual earnings and lower recidivism rates (Steurer & Smith, 2003). However, only 15% of inmates reported receiving educational programs that addressed their needs. Educational and job readiness programs may benefit partners and children if ex- offenders are more likely to find higher-paying and stable employment.

> *Educational and job readiness programs may benefit partners and children if ex-offenders are more likely to find higher-paying and stable employment.*

Substance abuse treatment is another aspect of correctional programming that bears relevance for family life.

Approximately 80% of inmates housed in state prison report a history of drug and/or alcohol use (Mumola, 1999). Substance abuse in the family is associated with poor parenting, parental conflict, and higher stress (Fals-Stewart, Birchler, & O'Farrell, 1996; Fals-Stewart, Kelley, Fincham, Golden, & Logsdon, 2004). Unfortunately, relapse after release is common. In the Returning Home Cleveland Study, Visher and Courtney (2007) found that 35% of the 300 men interviewed 1 year after release reported substance use. Men also reported that their substance abuse relapse was caused by relationship and family problems.

Interventions that treat drug abuse, particularly those that focus on the marital/partner relationship such as behavioral couples therapy (BCT), may hold promise for incarcerated husbands and fathers. In typical BCT treatment, the recovering client and his or her partner are seen for 15-20 outpatient sessions over the course of five to six months. BCT may also be conducted in a group format, with couples attending a series of 9-12 weekly sessions together. BCT with married and cohabitating couples (many of whom are referred through the criminal justice system) has been shown to lower intimate partner violence and substance use and improve dyadic adjustment and child well-being. It has been shown to be effective across a range of socioeconomic groups, as well as with racial and ethnic minority couples (Fals-Stewart et al., 2000; Kelley & Fals-Stewart, 2002; O'Farrell, Murphy, Stephan, Fals-Stewart, & Murphy, 2004).

Additionally, an evaluation of La Bodega de la Familia, a family- based program for inmates with substance abuse problems that is coordinated with pre- and post-release programming, found promising results for substance use and recidivism outcomes (Sullivan, Mino, Nelson & Pope, 2002; this example program is described in more detail in the box below).

Prison-based substance abuse treatment programs, particularly the therapeutic community intervention (TCI) approach, have been shown to be effective at improving substance use and recidivism outcomes following release. Knight, Simpson, & Hiller (1999) and Martin, Butzin, Saum, & Inciardi (1999) followed cohorts of incarcerated TCI participants in Texas and Delaware, respectively, and each found lower rates of re-arrest and reincarceration among treatment group members 3 years after release from prison, compared to comparison groups of similar inmates who did not participate in treatment. Butzin et al. (2002), analyzing data from the Delaware cohort, found that each component of the three-stage transitional treatment program (within prison, transitional, and aftercare) was associated with improved recidivism and relapse outcomes; however, the transitional residential component had the largest and most long-lasting treatment effects.

**Example Rehabilitation Program**

LA BODEGA DE LA FAMILIA (Sullivan, Mino, Nelson, & Pope, 2002)

La Bodega de la Familia, an experimental program in New York City, engages substance abusers and their family members in family case management and other services as a supplement to probation, parole, or pre-trial supervision. By providing support to the families of drug users in the criminal justice system, Bodega aims to increase the success of drug treatment, reduce the use of incarceration to punish relapse, and reduce the harms addiction causes within families.

To evaluate Bodega's impact, researchers compared outcomes for a sample of Bodega participants with outcomes for a comparison group of drug users and their family members. Researchers used standardized interview instruments that measure physical and mental health, family functioning, and social support when study members entered the research and again 6 months later. The researchers obtained official arrest and conviction data on each drug user in the study and conducted more detailed, ethnographic interviews with a subsample of both the Bodega participants and the comparison group.

Family members participating in the program obtained needed medical and social services at significantly higher rates than those in the comparison group, and they showed a significantly stronger sense of being supported emotionally and materially in their social relationships. At the same time, the percentage of Bodega substance abusers using any illegal drug declined from 80% to 42%, significantly more than in the comparison group. Arrests and convictions were also lower among drug users participating in Bodega more than 6 months. The reduction in drug use was not produced by greater use of drug treatment among Bodega participants, but instead appears to be a direct result of pressure and support from Bodega case managers and family members themselves. For more information, see Sullivan et al., 2002)

## 7.4. POST-RELEASE FAMILY PROGRAMS

To be effective, it is important to offer consistent support both during and after imprisonment. However, programs involving family during pre-release preparation and after release have been scarce and have been subject to limited evaluation (e.g., Bobbitt & Nelson, 2004). A thorough review of programs to assist with prisoners post-release did not include any that focused on partner or father-child relationships (Seiter & Kadela, 2003). Additionally, one study found that only 8% of fathers participated in parenting skills programs during the year after their release from prison (Visher & Courtney, 2007).

> *Family involvement in post-release programming is associated with decreased drug use, fewer physical and emotional problems, and decreased recidivism among fathers.*

Some research on family support programs after release has found that family involvement in programming is associated with positive outcomes, including decreased drug use; fewer mental, physical, and emotional problems; and decreased recidivism (Visher & Travis, 2003). As mentioned above, La Bodega de la Familia, which provided crisis intervention and case management services to drug abusers involved in the criminal justice system and their families through release, found reductions in drug use and recidivism and improvements in mental health functioning (Shapiro, 1999; Visher & Travis, 2003). Qualitative and quantitative interviews with 49 prisoners within the first month of their release indicated that families provided critical material (i.e., food, housing, and money) and emotional support, which was related to their post-release success in remaining drug-free and finding employment and stable housing (Nelson, Deess, & Allen, 1999). These studies indicate that it is important to involve families prior to release in order to put together a reentry plan (Bobbitt & Nelson, 2004; Festen et al., 2002). The family members typically involved in such programs have been parents, siblings, and other relatives of the offender; more effort is needed to involve spouses or intimate partners (Bobbitt & Nelson, 2004). For instance, Kaslow (1987) recommended addressing plans for reentry into family roles and relationships in the context of couples' therapy with incarcerated parents.

Further efforts to involve family in reentry and post-release programming are underway. For instance, Project Greenlight is a pilot program in New York City that involved four weeks of family reintegration sessions focused on couple, co-parenting, and family-of-origin relationships. Sessions were conducted by a family counselor during pre-release preparations, and have since been provided in the community after release (Bobbitt & Nelson, 2004). The Ohio Department of Rehabilitation and Correction is working to enhance family involvement in the continuum of incarceration, reentry, and post-release services by developing a Family Orientation Program at each reception center to provide information to families during incarceration, involving families in post-release supervision visits, and creating a Family Council to address family issues across the reentry continuum (La Vigne, Thomson, Visher, Kachnowski, & Travis, 2003). The Community Orientation and Reintegration (COR) program in Pennsylvania involves parenting education and reunification preparation during incarceration, individual and group counseling sessions around parenting skills and family strengths, and facilitation of family reunification in community corrections centers (La Vigne, Lawrence, Kachnowski, Naser, & Schaffer, 2002). Although process evaluations suggest that these programs are making strides toward meeting prisoners' needs for family involvement and reunification, outcome evaluations have not been conducted to assess the efficacy of such programs in promoting family strengthening and enhancing post-release success.

Other types of programs for returning prisoners and their families that may be applicable to marriage and family strengthening efforts include diversion programs that help fathers pay child support; faith-based programs that connect fathers to services upon release; support groups for fathers' partners; mentoring programs to support children of incarcerated fathers; and services that address more basic needs such as housing, food, and employment. Crossover between these efforts is needed to best support couples and families after fathers return to the community (Bauer et al., 2007).

## 7.5. RESEARCH LIMITATIONS

Most existing evaluations of prison-based parenting programs are limited by small sample sizes and brief follow-up periods, and all rely on self-report measures, which raise concerns about the social desirability of fathers' responses. A major research gap is understanding how to bring these programs to scale in criminal justice systems and preserve their implementation fidelity. Moreover, evaluations have generally not investigated program mediation to determine the pathways through which programs work and what core programmatic elements are most effective. Quantitative measures assessing intended outcomes over time are necessary to document program effectiveness. Evaluations of different types of programs, including individual and group counseling around parenting issues, are needed. Program evaluations need to include larger and more diverse samples as well as assessments of children and other caregivers. Future work should also examine the mediating role of parenting practices in program effects on child well-being.

Almost no research has examined the effectiveness of family strengthening programs for fathers across the reentry period. Beyond program descriptions and estimates of the number of families that participate, there is little evidence that efforts to improve partner and father-child relationships upon reentry and after release have positive implications for father or family wellbeing or reentry and post-release success. Future work should build on the research that has evaluated the efficacy of prison- based family strengthening programs and the scant evaluation research on programs like La Bodega de la Familia. Specifically needed are studies that randomly assign reentering fathers and their families to relationship enhancement programs versus control groups and follow them over time to assess outcomes. Moreover, it is important to conduct evaluations of programs currently implemented in several states that begin during incarceration and continue after release, as this approach is predicted to yield the most positive outcomes (Bobbitt & Nelson, 2004).

*Chapter 8*

# CHALLENGES TO IMPLEMENTING FAMILY STRENGTHENING PROGRAMS IN PRISON AND AT REENTRY

Numerous challenges to program implementation have been identified that apply to both marriage education and parenting programs during incarceration and after reentry. Cooperation between criminal justice and community-based human service agencies, family involvement, participant recruitment and retention, stigma, and cultural competence are some of the obstacles facing family strengthening programs targeting incarcerated men and their partners and children.

## 8.1. BUILDING PARTNERSHIPS WITH COMMUNITY-BASED ORGANIZATIONS

In a broad sense, correctional and human service agencies often have different roles and priorities that can impede the implementation of family strengthening efforts with incarcerated and reentering fathers (Festen et al., 2002; Nurse, 2004; Rossman, 2001). Correctional institutions prioritize public safety, which carries an emphasis on controlling all movements and activities within their facilities for the protection of inmates, staff, visitors, and the public (Lawrence et al., 2002). Human services agencies, by contrast, emphasize meeting the needs of their clients, which necessitates a focus on individual well-being and self-determination (Rossman, 2001). Whereas corrections policies attempt to encourage responsible behavior by imposing penalties on offenders, fatherhood policies encourage fathers to take responsibility for their children and suggest programming that support this goal. These approaches can come into conflict with one another, for instance discouraging efforts to pay child support by deepening fathers' debt while in prison (Nurse, 2004) or impeding fathers' ability to stay connected with their children by limiting contact and visitation while in prison (Jeffries et al., 2001).

> *Correctional institutions' emphasis on safety and control and human service agencies' focus on client support may clash during service integration.*

Because most prison-based programs are provided by external community-based organizations (CBOs) that focus on service provision, it is necessary for these organizations to build partnerships with correctional and probation/parole agencies and to develop a shared vision of the program. Support for family programs must be secured from the corrections systems and personnel, including state-level officials, facility superintendents, and correctional officers, in order to promote successful implementation (Adalist-Estrin, 1994; Eddy et al., 2001; Jeffries et al., 2001), but corrections facilities have been generally unsupportive of family-oriented services (Eddy et al., 2001). Correctional institutions need to be willing to open their facilities to outside organizations (Rossman, 2001), but it may be difficult for CBO staff to gain entry to correctional facilities due to lengthy background checks and limited time and space availability. Prison rules may also be enforced inconsistently or without obvious rationale, which can be challenging for outside staff (Jeffries et al., 2001). Additionally, elements of programs such as content, activities, duration, location, and number of participants may be limited by constraints of the prison environment and policies as well as the strong emphasis on prisoner security (Jeffries et al., 2001). On the other hand, community-based service agencies are often located far from prisons and may not consider inmates as potential clients or may not be aware of services available for inmates (Rossman, 2001). In addition, partnerships between CBOs and correctional agencies often create numerous record-keeping and information-sharing challenges, as data-sharing agreements are difficult to establish and correctional agencies typically do not have staff time designated for generating reports or other information to be shared with CBOs delivering programs (Rossman, 2001). Staff turnover at correctional facilities and CBOs also makes the maintenance of stable partnerships and the delivery of consistent programming difficult (Lawrence et al., 2002). Thus, more coordination between corrections agencies and the organizations responsible for implementing family strengthening programs could improve the quality of prison-based programs. For instance, one approach that could facilitate understanding and buy-in is for program development and delivery staff to provide presentations to corrections staff regarding project rationale and activities (Eddy et al., 2001).

## 8.2. BARRIERS TO FAMILY INVOLVEMENT

Correctional agencies' inherent emphasis on security and safety also creates barriers to involving family members in programming delivered within prison walls. Any contact or exchange of information between incarcerated individuals and non-incarcerated individuals is potentially problematic from a security standpoint and requires monitoring by correctional staff, which, in a time of increased prisoner populations and decreasing funding for prison staffing, has the potential to strain both budgets and individual staff members (Lawrence et al., 2002). Facility staff may view family members as both an inconvenience and a threat to security; as a result, they are less likely to be encouraging of new programs that bring family members into the prison, and may treat participants in existing family programs in a manner that subtly discourages their continued participation (Bobbit and Nelson, 2004).

*Geographic distance from prison, busy schedules, and tenuous relationships serve as barriers to family involvement in prison programs.*

Tenuous relationships between incarcerated fathers and their partners may cause partners to be reluctant about attending relationship programs (Nurse, 2004). Relationships are also likely to dissolve over time while fathers are incarcerated (Holt & Miller, 1972), so recruiting of couples in relationship education or counseling programs may be challenging. Additionally, partners and spouses often live far away from the prison facility, making it difficult to deliver services to them (Bobbitt & Nelson, 2004). Mothers often have busy schedules around employment and childcare that prison programs cannot always accommodate (Bobbitt & Nelson, 2004; Markman et al., 2005). Partners also may have criminal histories which preclude their visitation to prisons. Supports and incentives that mitigate these barriers, such as free childcare, transportation support, food, or small monetary incentives, are likely to improve recruitment and retention of family members in programming (Coatsworth, Duncan, Pantin, & Szapocznik, 2006).

Furthermore, it is often difficult to recruit children to participate in programs with their fathers, because their mothers or caregivers are required to consent and provide transportation and may not be supportive of the father having a relationship with the child (Hairston, 2001; Palm, 2001). As with partners, children's school or activity schedules may not coincide with the available times for program activities (Bobbitt & Nelson, 2004). This may limit opportunities for fathers to apply the knowledge they gain in programs to interactions with their children (Harrison, 1997). Thus, an important next step is to investigate approaches to delivering marriage and parenting programs that address some of these barriers. Even if barriers prevent partner involvement, research suggests that marital education programs delivered to prisoners without their spouses may still have beneficial impacts on their relationship attitudes and skills (Kaslow, 1987).

## 8.3. RECRUITMENT AND RETENTION OF INCARCERATED PARTICIPANTS

Participant recruitment and retention are also challenges in prison- and community-based family support programs of any type. Given the competing programs in which prisoners may participate, such as work release programs or substance abuse treatment, they may feel that family strengthening programs are less important or not relevant to them (Bobbitt & Nelson, 2004). Many inmates cannot afford to spend unpaid time in training and educational programs after release (Jeffries et al., 2001). Inmates may also be skeptical of programs that involve discussions about sensitive family-related topics (Eddy et al., 2001). Large numbers of inmate transfers between facilities, early releases, frequent residential moves upon release, the likelihood of reincarceration, and the fragility of family relationships make retention and follow-up evaluation difficult (Eddy et al., 2001; Palm, 2001; Meek, 2007). It is also important to identify appropriate participants for family strengthening programs. Some men may not be ready to participate in such programs due to a previous history of domestic violence or child abuse (Bobbitt & Nelson, 2004; Palm, 2001). Other men have mental disorders and limited reading ability, both of which may inhibit their ability to comprehend program materials (Eddy et al., 2001).

*Large numbers of inmate transfers between facilities, early releases, frequent residential moves upon release, the likelihood of reincarceration, and the fragility of family relationships make retention and follow-up evaluation difficult.*

Additionally, the demands placed on released fathers to attend court hearings, parole appearances, and other appointments may limit their ability to participate in programs in the community (Jeffries et al., 2001).

Agencies need to develop strategies for identifying and recruiting participants, either while they are in prison or after they are released. Strategies may include referrals from corrections or parole departments or from other programs such as substance abuse treatment centers. Staff offering prison- based programs could recruit inmates directly by providing presentations about project topics along with referral forms for participation (Eddy et al., 2001). Incentives could be provided for participation, such as small monetary payment, additional free time, or family visitation privileges. Outside of prisons, it may be a challenge to identify large numbers of reentering fathers in a given geographic area. Once participants are recruited, developing a tracking form for each person may improve follow-up with additional services and evaluation activities (Eddy et al., 2001).

## 8.4. STIGMA IN GROUP SETTING

As most family strengthening programs in prison take place in a group setting, they face barriers related to stigmatization. Asking men to share their thoughts, in a group setting, on difficult issues involving their children is a challenge (Palm, 2001). Pressure to be unemotional or to disrespect ex-partners may interfere with fathers' ability to express their actual feelings about fatherhood or relationships. One program has reduced stigma by establishing ground rules and using icebreakers (Palm, 2001). Program implementers should continue to address fathers' perceptions that participating in such programs indicates that they are weak or have family problems.

## 8.5. CONNECTING WITH SUPPORTIVE SERVICES POST RELEASE

It is important for released prisoners to continue participation in family strengthening programs and other social services after reentry (Bobbitt & Nelson, 2004; Kaslow, 1987; Meek, 2007). Continued participation may help encourage the use of knowledge and skills gained while incarcerated. Yet, prisoners are often released without links to community-based services. Human service agencies often have little connection with the criminal justice system and do not have formal mechanisms for sharing information about families in need. Resources may not be available to support community-based service delivery due to costs and uncertain release dates. Furthermore, inadequate understanding of post-release assistance entitlement can make transition planning difficult, and paperwork involved in connecting offenders with services in the community can be cumbersome and can take months to process (Rossman, 2001). Other barriers include lack of service coordination between community- and prison-based services due to long distances between the prison and the community where the family resides (and/or to which to prisoner plans to return) and different funding streams for programming within and outside of the correctional system (Bobbitt & Nelson, 2004; Rossman, 2001).

> *Providing a strategy to continue supportive services after release is crucial.*

Ironically, many incarcerated fathers and their families come from disadvantaged communities that are involved with both the criminal justice and health and human services systems (Festen et al., 2002). Thus, more attention should be paid to how these disparate systems can intersect in disadvantaged communities to better meet the needs of families through improved service delivery.

There are a few existing parenting programs that connect fathers with services in the community, such as job training, in order to prepare for reentry (Bowling, 1999; Jeffries et al., 2001). For instance, the Nontraditional Opportunities for Work (NOW) project represents a partnership between the Wisconsin Department of Correction and the Department of Workforce Development. This project combines support in areas such as parenting skills, child support, and paternity with assistance finding stable employment though training, education, and other services (Festen et al., 2002). Similarly, the Montgomery County Pre-release Center in Maryland provides information and training on employment in addition to guidance on parenting and family relationships (Jeffries et al., 2001). However, the impacts of such efforts on reentry success have yet to be evaluated.

## 8.6. CULTURAL SENSITIVITY

Although a high percentage of incarcerated fathers are of ethnic minorities, very few family strengthening programs in prison or surrounding reentry have been designed with cultural issues in mind. Those programs that have addressed culture have reported positive reactions from participants. For instance, one program uses discussion of family traditions and rituals, and videos and literature depicting different cultural groups, in order to make sure that program content resonates with a variety of fathers (Palm, 2001). Another program found it helpful to hire a facilitator of the same ethnicity as the participants (LaRosa & Rank, 2001). The implications of these efforts for program success have not been evaluated, and there is little theoretical development to guide research testing the impact of culturally relevant program content on inmate outcomes.

In the future, programs that aim to strengthen partner and father-child relationships need to be sensitive to cultural differences in family relationship definitions, expectations, and behaviors (Adalist-Estrin, 1994; Bauer et al., 2007; Meek, 2007; Palm, 2001). Qualitative research could aim to identify programmatic approaches and activities that would be culturally relevant and acceptable among different groups. Using this information, programs could be tailored to the diversity of prison populations, and evaluation of these programs would be necessary to test their effectiveness.

## 8.7. RESEARCH LIMITATIONS

Several challenges to the implementation of marriage and family strengthening programs in prison and upon reentry have been identified, and many recommendations for improving implementation have been made based on descriptive and anecdotal information. Identification of challenges has rarely involved actual surveys of program or correctional staff. Research has not tested the extent to which the identified barriers to implementation impact the effectiveness of programs, nor the extent to which addressing different barriers to program implementation in turn improves the impacts of program participation for incarcerated and reentering fathers and their families.

Experimental manipulation of implementation conditions would be difficult in some situations. However, it would be possible to randomly assign some corrections staff to receive training and technical assistance in connecting family strengthening programs to other initiatives and increasing institutional support for such programs in order to determine whether addressing such issues is associated with increased program efficacy. Alternatively, fathers could be randomly assigned to participate in different programs with varying levels of evidence bases or cultural tailoring. There are many dimensions along which programs and their contexts could be varied in order to conduct more rigorous research on implementation challenges and how they can be overcome.

An additional limitation of research on family strengthening programs with incarcerated fathers is a lack of understanding with regards to the steps involved in making such programs sustainable and encouraging widespread dissemination. Presumably, the implementation challenges identified above, including lack of support of programs by corrections staff, restrictions in the prison setting that limit program flexibility, and lack of coordination between corrections and human services in reentry programming, may also impede the assumption of ownership of programs within correctional facilities and agencies, which would be the most direct way to enhance sustainability. However, it is possible that the development of long-term relationships between corrections agencies and community service providers could facilitate sharing of resources and strategies to obtain further resources to continue program implementation. Challenges to recruitment and retention will also need to be addressed in order to involve enough participants to ensure sustainability. Moreover, once effective programs are identified, research should test whether such programs can be replicated in different settings with varying populations and with lower levels of control over implementation, in an effort to determine which programs can be disseminated to reach larger numbers of incarcerated fathers and their families.

As family strengthening programs in prisons continue to be evaluated, it will be important to learn from the challenges that are faced and the solutions that are found. New approaches to serving incarcerated fathers, their partners, and their children may illuminate ways to successfully reach this population and help to enhance their fragile relationships.

# Chapter 9

# CONCLUSIONS

This report documents the state of the extant research on incarceration and family life. Our goal was to provide a timely and evidence-based summary of the research in order to document what we known about the effects of father incarceration on family life and to illuminate some next steps in research, policy, and programming for the field.

Our review yields consistent themes that incarceration harms opportunities for marriage, increases the likelihood of marital/partner dissolution, and lessens the chances of father involvement. Women separated from their partners experience a host of daunting tasks, which may include single parenting; subsisting on a diminished income; facing social stigma, loneliness, and isolation; and dealing with the emotional turmoil of having a loved one incarcerated. Children may face similarly challenging ordeals, including feelings of abandonment, economic deprivation, changes in caregivers and residence, and increases in emotional problems.

The reentry process is also marked by challenging family reintegration issues. The hardships of recreating life after prison and reestablishing family roles can strain emotional resources. Reconnecting with children after long separations is a difficult process. Yet, success in these endeavors has important implications for recidivism and family well-being. Our review of the literature suggests that access to family strengthening programs is often inconsistent and insufficient.

However, promising approaches are emerging. Although sparse and sporadic, correctional facilities are beginning to offer marriage education classes, couples counseling, and furlough programs for partners to reconnect. Imprisoned men are slowly gaining access to parenting support, including group classes, group therapy, and increased and enhanced visitation. There approaches focus on essential relationship skills such as communication, emotional understanding, problem-solving, conflict resolution, and affection and intimacy. These programs aim to increase father involvement and parental efficacy by enhancing understanding of child development, discipline techniques, anger management, the importance of fatherhood, and co-parenting relationships.

Although these programs have consistently been dogged by a lack of rigorous evaluation, preliminary evidence is accumulating that indicates the potential of these programs to improve partner and parenting relationships. Evaluations of marriage/partner interventions in prison suggest that they can be successful in increasing communication skills and relationship satisfaction and decreasing negative couple interactions, feelings of loneliness, and recidivism. Prison-based parenting programs have shown achievements in skill building and perceptions regarding the importance of involved fatherhood. Moreover, fathers involved in these parenting programs have reported increased contacts with children.

Despite these successes, a number of barriers still exist that limit service provision and retention, including lack of partnerships between the criminal justice system and community-based organizations and difficulties in involving family members because of geographic distance and time constraints.

The most striking finding of our literature review is the lack of rigorous research aimed at fully understanding and serving incarcerated fathers and their families. To summarize the issues faced by the women and children affected by men's incarceration, we relied on a relatively small body of research. These sources mainly included small, qualitative research studies that involved interviews or focus groups with men who were in prison or were recently released and with their spouse/partner. These studies relied on nonrepresentative groups of individuals and, thus we cannot say with any certainty that the issues they face are generalizable to the diverse inmate population. Although these studies have been important for identifying issues likely faced by most inmates and their families, more research is imperative to investigate the processes through which imprisonment affects marriage, child adjustment, and community collective efficacy. Moreover, with a few notable exceptions, much of the research is not longitudinal. What is critically needed is research that follows individuals and their families throughout the period of criminal justice involvement to examine (1) how key points such as the arrest and trial, incarceration, and release affect families; (2) the mechanisms through which individuals and families deal with these stressors; and (3) the factors that are associated with successful coping and adaptation. The identification of theory-based and empirically derived risk and protective factors is key to the development of effective interventions. However, in order to disentangle the effects of incarceration from those of other risk factors that accompany it, including poverty, substance abuse, family violence, and racial discrimination, what is needed is longitudinal research that includes a comparison group of similar individuals and their families not involved in the criminal justice system.

The literature available to support evidence-based approaches to family strengthening is also limited by the lack of rigorous evaluation methods. Those who do include evaluations often have small, nonrepresentative samples, single group pre- and post-test designs (i.e., no control or comparison groups), and brief follow-up periods that rely on data from a single reporter. Rigorous experimental or quasi-experimental evaluation efforts are needed to identify approaches that work best. The field will benefit greatly from the use of the strongest research designs to justify social policies and intervention services.

To advance the research base, a stronger focus on cultural diversity is also necessary. Men of color are overrepresented in the criminal justice system, and communities of color pay a high price for incarceration including decreased family stability, limited father involvement in child-rearing and reduced family income. Research is needed that explores cultural roots, community contexts, and the diversity of family and kinship patterns and how they can be strengthened when a family member is imprisoned. Moreover, it is important to recognize that interventions and policies may work differently for individuals of varied cultural backgrounds; thus, research that examines how race/ethnicity moderates intervention effectiveness is critical. Finally, researchers and policy makers need to carefully scrutinize policy interventions to ensure that they are not leading to unanticipated negative consequences. For instance, services that promote marital commitment need to ensure that women and children are not unintentionally exposed to family violence and abuse in the attempt to reintegrate ex-offenders back into their nuclear family.

Despite these limitations, research and practice in this area is moving forward. Evaluations of multi-site and community grant programs are currently underway which will shed light on best practices for the field. The national multi-site evaluation of recipients of the Marriage and Family Strengthening Grants for Incarcerated Fathers and Their Partners will yield critical information about the types of program, policies, and strategies that are most effective in enhancing healthy marriages and supporting responsible fatherhood. This large-scale evaluation and other smaller research efforts currently underway will help elucidate how successful programs work and for whom they work best. An important facet of this work will be to identify practices that facilitate coordination between human service and criminal justice agencies and suggest how institutional and organizational policies can smooth the way for future efforts to strengthen families facing parental incarceration. More evidence will help ensure that our social policies are having the intended outcomes of reducing recidivism and improving family functioning and child well-being.

# REFERENCES

Accordino, M. P., & Guerney, B. (1998). An evaluation of the relationship enhancement program with prisoners and their wives. *Journal of Offender Therapy and Comparative Criminology, 42*(1), 5-15.

Adalist-Estrin, A. (1994). Family support and criminal justice. In S. L. Kagan & B. Weissbound (Eds.), *Putting families first: America's family support movement and the challenge of change* (pp. 161-185). San Francisco, CA: Jossey- Bass.

Amato, P. R. (2005). The impact of family formation change on the cognitive, social and emotional well-being of the next generation, *Future Child, 15*(2), 75-96.

Arditti, J. A. (2005). Families and incarceration: An ecological approach. *Families in Society: Journal of Contemporary Social Services, 86*(2), 251-260.

Arditti, J. A., Lambert-Shute, J., & Joest, K. (2003). Saturday morning at the jail: Implications of incarceration for families and children. *Family Relations, 52*, 195-204.

Babcock, J. C., & La Taillade, J. J. (2000). Evaluating interventions for men who batter. In J. P. Vincent & E. N. Jouriles (Eds.), *Domestic violence: Guidelines for research-informed practice* (pp. 37–77). Philadelphia, PA: Jessica Kingsley Publishers.

Babcock, J. C., Waltz, J., Jacobson, N. S., & Gottman, J. M. (1993). Power and violence: The relation between communication patterns, power discrepancies, and domestic violence. *Journal of Consulting and Clinical Psychology, 61*, 40-50.

Baer, D., Bhati, A., Brooks, L., Castro, J., La Vigne, N., Mallik-Kane, K., Naser, R., et al. (2005). *Understanding the challenges of prisoner reentry: Research findings from the Urban Institute's prisoner reentry portfolio.* Washington, DC: Urban Institute.

Bahr, S. J., Armstrong, A. H., Gibbs, B. G., Harris, P. E., & Fisher, J. K. (2005). The reentry process: How parolees adjust to release from prison. *Fathering, 3,* 243-265.

Bauer, B., Hart, J., Hopewell, A., & Tein, N. (2007). *Research and practice symposium on marriage and incarceration: A meeting summary.* Health Systems Research, Inc.

Baunach, P. J. (1985). *Mothers in prison.* New Brunswick, NJ: Transaction, Inc.

Bayse, D. J., Allgood, S. M., & Van Wyk, P. H. (1991). Family life education: An effective tool for prisoner rehabilitation. *Family Relations, 40*(3), 254-257.

Bernard, S., & Knitzer, J. (1999). *Map and track: State initiatives to encourage responsible fatherhood.* New York: National Center for Children in Poverty, Columbia University Mailman Center School of Public Health. Retrieved November 12, 2007, from http://www.nccp.org/publications/ pdf/ text_439.pdf.

Bobbitt, M., & Nelson, M. (2004). *The front line: Building programs that recognize families' role in reentry.* New York: Vera Institute of Justice. Retrieved October 1, 2007, from http://www.vera.org/publication_pdf/ 249_476 . pdf.

Bowling, G. (1999). The MELD for young dads program. *Family and Corrections Network Report, 20,* 10-11.

Braman, D., & Wood, J. (2003). From one generation to the next: How criminal sanctions are reshaping family life in urban America. In J. Travis & M. Waul (Eds.), *Prisoners once removed* (pp. 157-188). Washington, DC: The Urban Institute Press.

Brenner, E. (1999). Fathers in prison: A review of the data. *Family and Corrections Network Report, 20,* 3-7.

Bronte-Tinkew, J., Carrano, J., Allen, T., Bowie, L., Mbawa, K., & Matthews, G. (2007). *Elements of promising practice for fatherhood programs: Evidence-based research findings on programs for fathers.* Retrieved June 9, 2008, from http://basis.caliber.com/cwig/ws/library/docs/fatherhd/ Blob/62423 .pdf?rpp=- 10&upp=0&m= 1&w=NATIVE%28%27TI+ph+is+%27% 27 Elements+of+ Promising+ Practice+for+ Fatherhood+ Pr ograms+%3A+ Evidence-Based+ Research + Findings+on + Programs+for+ Fathers %27%27%27%29&r= 1&order=native%28%27year%2F Descend%27%29

Bureau of Justice Statistics (BJS) (2000). *Compendium of Federal Justice Statistics.* Washington, DC: U.S. Department of Justice. Retrieved June 29, 2006, from http://www.ojp.usdoj.gov/bjs/abstract/cfjs00.htm.

Bureau of Justice Statistics (BJS) (2008). *Jail Statistics.* Washington, DC: U.S. Department of Justice. Retrieved August 27, 2008, from http://www.ojp.usdoj.gov/bjs/jails.htm.

Bureau of Justice Statistics (BJS) (2008). *Prison Statistics.* Washington, DC: U.S. Department of Justice. Retrieved August 25, 2008, from http://www.ojp.usdoj.gov/bjs/prisons.htm.

Bureau of Justice Statistics (BJS) (2008). *Probation and Parole Statistics.* Washington, DC: U.S. Department of Justice. Retrieved August 25, 2008, from http://www.ojp.usdoj.gov/bjs/pandp.htm.

Butzin, C. A., Martin, S. S., & Inciardi, J. A. (2002). Evaluating component effects of a prison-based treatment continuum. *Journal of Substance Abuse Treatment, 22*, 63-69.

Carlson, B. E., & Cervera, N. (1992). *Inmates and their wives: Incarceration and family life.* Westport, CT: Greenwood Press.

Clayton, O., & Moore, J. (2003). The effects of crime and imprisonment on family formation. In O. Clayton, R. B. Mincy, and D. Blankenhorn (Eds.), *Black Fathers in Contemporary American Society: Strengths, Weaknesses, and Strategies for Change.* Russell Sage Foundation: New York.

Coatsworth, J. D., Duncan, L. G., Pantin, H., & Szapocznik, J. (2006). Patterns of retention in a preventive intervention with ethnic minority families. *Journal of Primary Prevention, 27*(2), 17 1–193.

Conway, T., & Hutson, R.Q. (2007). Parental incarceration: How to avoid a "death sentence" for families. *Journal of Law and Public Policy Clearinghouse Review, 41*(3-4), 2 14-22 1.

Coombs, R. H. (1991). Marital status and personal well-being: A literature review. *Family Relations, 40*, 97-102.

Cornille, T. A., Barlow, L. O., & Cleveland, A. D. (2005). DADS family project: An experiential group approach to support fathers in their relationships with their children. *Social Work with Groups, 28*, 41-57.

Day, R., Acock, A., Bahr, S., & Arditti, J. (2005). Incarcerated fathers returning home to children and families: Introduction to the special issue and a primer on doing research with men in prison. *Fathering, 3*(3), 183-200.

Department of Labor (2007). *About PRI.* Retrieved September 3, 2008, from http://www.doleta.gov/pri/aboutPRI.cfm.

Doherty, W. J., & Anderson, J. R. (2004). Community marriage initiatives. *Family Relations, 53*(5), 425-432.

Dunn, E., & Arbuckle, J. G. (2002). *Children of incarcerated parents and enhanced visitation programs: Impacts of the Living Interactive Family Education (LIFE) Program. University of Missouri Extension.* Retrieved October 1, 2007, from http://extension.missouri.edu/crp/l ifeeval uation/LIFEreport.doc.

Eddy, B. A., Powell, M. J., Szubka, M. H., McCool, M. L., & Kuntz, S. (2001). Challenges in research with incarcerated parents and importance in violence prevention. *American Journal of Preventive Medicine, 20,* 56-62.

Eddy, J. M., & Reid, J. B. (2003). The adolescent children of incarcerated parents: A developmental perspective. In J. Travis & M. Waul (Eds.), *Prisoners once removed* (pp. 233-258). Washington, DC: The Urban Institute Press.

Edin, K. (2000). Few good men: Why poor mothers don't marry or remarry. *The American Prospect, 11,* 26-31.

Edin, K., Nelson, T. J., & Paranal, R. (2001). Fatherhood and incarceration as potential turning points in the criminal careers of unskilled men. Evanston, IL: Northwestern University Institute for Policy Research. Retrieved September 3, 2008 from http://www.northwestern.edu/ipr/publications/ papers/2 001/fatherhood. pdf.

Fals-Stewart, W., Birchler, G. R., & Kelley, M. L. (2006). Learning sobriety together: A randomized clinical trial examining behavioral couples therapy with alcoholic female patients. *Journal of Consulting and Clinical Psychology, 74,* 579-591.

Fals-Stewart, W., Birchler, G. R., & O'Farrell, T. J. (1996). Behavioral couples therapy for male substance-abusing patients: Effects on relationship adjustment and drug- using behavior. *Journal of Consulting and Clinical Psychology, 64*(5), 959-972.

Fals-Stewart, W., Kelley, M. L., Fincham, F. D., Golden, J., & Logsdon, T. (2004). Emotional and behavioral problems of children living with drug-abusing fathers: Comparisons of children living with alcohol-abusing and non-substance-abusing fathers. *Journal of Family Psychology, 18,* 19–330.

Fals-Stewart, W., O'Farrell, T. J., Feehan, M., Birchler, G. R., Tiller, S., & McFarlin, S. K. (2000). Behavioral couples therapy versus individual-based treatment for male substance-abusing patients: An evaluation of significant individual change and comparison of improvement rates. *Journal of Substance Abuse Treatment, 18*(3), 249-254.

Family Strengthening Policy Center (2005). Policy brief no. 12. November.

Festen, M., Waul, M., Solomon, A., & Travis, J. (2002). *From prison to home: The effect of incarceration and reentry on children, families and communities.*

*Conference report.* Washington, DC: U.S. Department of Health and Human Services.

Fishman, L. T. (1990). *Women at the wall: A study of prisoners' wives doing time on the outside.* Albany, NY: State University of New York Press.

Fursten berg, F. F. (1995). Fathering in the inner city: Paternal participation and public policy. In W. Marsiglio (Ed.), *Fatherhood: Contemporary theory, research and public policy* (pp. 119-147). Thousand Oaks, CA: Sage Publications.

Gibson-Davis, C. M., Edin, K., & McLanahan, S. (2005). High hopes but even higher expectations: The retreat from marriage among low-income couples. *Journal of Marriage and Family, 67,* 1301-1312.

Glaze, L. E., & Maruschak, L. M. (2008). Parents in prison and their minor children. *Bureau of Justice Statistics Special Report.* Washington, DC: Bureau of Justice Statistics.

Glueck, S., & Glueck, E. (1950). *Unraveling juvenile delinquency.* New York: The Commonwealth Fund.

Griswold, E., & Pearson, J. (2003). Twelve reasons for collaboration between departments of correction and child-support enforcement agencies. *Corrections Today, 65,* 87-95.

Hagan, J., & Dinovitzer, R. (1999). Collateral consequences of imprisonment for children, communities, and prisoners. *Crime and Justice, 26,* 121-162.

Hairston, C. F. (1988). Family ties during imprisonment: Do they influence future criminal activity? *Federal Probation, 52*(1), 48-52.

Hairston, C. F. (1998). The forgotten parent: Understanding the forces that influence incarcerated fathers' relationships with their children. *Child Welfare, 77,* 617-639.

Hairston, C. F. (2001). Fathers in prison: Responsible fatherhood and responsible public policies. *Marriage and Family Review, 32,* 111-126.

Hairston, C. F. (2008). *Focus on children with incarcerated parents: An overview of the research literature.* Baltimore, MD: The Annie E. Casey Foundation.

Hairston, C. F., & Lockett, P. W. (1987). Parents in prison: New directions for social services. *Social Work, 32,* 162-164.

Hairston, C. F., & Oliver, W. (2006). *Safe return: Domestic violence and prisoner reentry: Experiences of Black women and men.* New York: Vera Institute of Justice. Retrieved October 19, 2007 from http://www.vera.org/publications/ publications_5.asp?pu blication_id =367.

Hairston, C. F., Rollin, J., & Jo, H. (2004). *Family connections during imprisonment and prisoners' community reentry.* Chicago, IL: University of

Chicago. Retrieved October 19, 2007, from http://www.uic.edu/jaddams/college/fami lycon nections. pdf.

Haney, C. (2001). *The psychological impact of incarceration: Implications for post-prison adjustment.* Santa Cruz, CA: University of California. Retrieved from http://aspe.hhs.gov/search/hsp/prison2home02/Haney. htm.

Harrison, K. (1997). Parental training for incarcerated fathers: Effects on attitudes, self-esteem, and children's self- perception. *Journal of Social Psychology, 137*(5), 588- 593.

Healey, K., Smith, C., & O'Sullivan, C. (1998). *Batterer intervention: Program approaches and criminal justice strategies.* U.S. Department of Justice, Office of Justice Programs, National Institute of Justice. Retrieved from http://www.ncjrs.gov/pdffiles/168638.pdf

Holt, N., & Miller, D. (1972). Explorations in inmate-family relationships. *Family and Corrections Network Report, 46.*

Howser, J., & MacDonald, D. (1982). Maintaining family ties. *Corrections Today, 44,* 96-98.

Huebner, B. M. (2005). The effect of incarceration on marriage and work over the life course. *Justice Quarterly, 22*(3), 282-303.

Huebner, B. M. (2007). Racial and ethnic differences in the likelihood of marriage: The effect of incarceration. *Justice Quarterly, 24*(1), 156-183.

Hughes, M. (1998). Turning points in the lives of young inner- city men forgoing destructive criminal behaviors: A qualitative study. *Social Work Research, 22,* 143-151.

Hughes, M. J., & Harrison-Thompson, J. (2002). Prison parenting programs: A national survey. *The Social Policy Journal, 1,* 57-74.

Jeffries, J. M., Menghraj, S., & Hairston, C. F. (2001). *Serving incarcerated and ex-offender fathers and their families: A review of the field.* New York: Vera Institute of Justice. Retrieved October 1, 2007, from http://www.vera.org/publication_pdf/fathers. PDF.

Jewkes, R. (2002). Intimate partner violence: causes and prevention. *The Lancet, 359,* 1423-1429.

Johnson, E. (2006). Youth with incarcerated parents: An introduction to the issues. *The Prevention Researcher, 13*(2), 1-6.

Johnson, E., & Waldfogel, J. (2002). *Children of incarcerated parents: Cumulative risks and children's living arrangements.* Joint Center for Policy Research Working Paper. New York: Columbia University. Retrieved October 2, 2007, from http://www.jcpr.org/wpfiles/ johnson_waldfogel.pdf?CFID=53947 1&CFTOKEN =43733 412.

Johnson, M. (1995). Patriarchal terrorism and common couple violence: two forms of violence against women. *Journal of Marriage and the Family, 57*, 283-294.

Johnston, D. (1991). *Jailed mothers*. Pasadena, CA: Pacific Oaks Center for Children of Incarcerated Parents.

Johnston, D. (2006). The wrong road: Efforts to understand the effects of parental crime and incarceration. *Criminology and Public Policy, 5*(4), 703-720.

Johnston, D. (1995). Effects of parental incarceration. In K. Gabel & D. Johnston (Eds.), *Children of incarcerated parents* (pp. 59-88). New York: Lexington Books.

Jorgensen, J. D., Hernandez, S. H., & Warren, R. C. (1986). Addressing the social needs of families of prisoners: A tool for inmate rehabilitation. *Federal Probation, 50*, 47- 52.

Jose-Kampfner, C. (1995). Post-traumatic stress reactions of children of imprisoned mothers. In K. Gabel and D. Johnston (Eds.), *Children of incarcerated parents* (pp. 89-100). New York: Lexington Books.

Kaslow, F. W. (1987). Couples or family therapy for prisoners and their significant others. *The American Journal of Family Therapy, 15*, 352-360.

Kelley, M. L., & Fals-Stewart, W. (2002). Couples- versus individual-based therapy for alcohol and drug abuse: Effects on children's psychosocial functioning. *Journal of Consulting and Clinical Psychology, 70*(2), 417-427.

Kinner, S. A., Alati, R., Najman, J. M., & Williams, G. M. (2007). Do paternal arrest and imprisonment lead to child behavior problems and substance use? A longitudinal analysis. *Journal of Child Psychology and Psychiatry, 48*(11), 1148-1156.

Knight K., Simpson D. D., & Hiller, M. L. (1999). Three-year reincarceration outcomes for in-prison therapeutic community treatment in Texas. *Prison Journal, 79.* 337– 351.

Landreth, G. L., & Lobaugh, A. F. (1998). Filial therapy with incarcerated fathers: Effects on parental acceptance of child, parental stress, and child adjustment. *Journal of Counseling and Development, 76*, 157-165.

Lanier, C. S. (1991). Dimensions of father-child interaction in a New York State prison population. *Journal of Offender Rehabilitation, 16*(3/4), 27-42.

Lanier, C. S. (1993). Affective states of fathers in prison. *Justice Quarterly, 10*, 49-66.

LaRosa, J. J., & Rank, M. G. (2001). Parenting education and incarcerated fathers. *Journal of Family Social Work, 6*, 15-33.

Larson, J. H. (2004). Innovations in marriage education: Introduction and challenges. *Family Relations, 53*, 421- 424.

Laub, J. H., Nagin, D. S., & Sampson, R. J. 1998. Trajectories of change in criminal offending: Good marriages and the desistance process. *American Sociological Review, 63,* 225-238.

La Vigne, N. G., Lawrence, S., Kachnowski, V., Naser, R., & Schaffer, M. (2002). *Process evaluation of the Pennsylvania Community Orientation and Reintegration (COR) program.* Washington, DC: The Urban Institute, Justice Policy Center.

La Vigne, N. G., Thomson, G. L., Visher, C., Kachnowski, V., & Travis, J. (2003). A portrait of prisoner reentry in Ohio. Washington, DC: Urban Institute.

Lawrence, S., Mears, D. P., Dubin, G., & Travis, J. (2002). *The practice and promise of prison programming.* Washington, DC: Urban Institute.

LeClair, D. P. & Guarino-Ghezzi, S. (1991). Does incapacitation guarantee public safety? Lessons from the Massachusetts furlough and prerelease programs. *Justice Quarterly, 8*(1), 9–36.

Levingston, K.D. & Turetsky, V. (2007). Debtors' prison: Prisoners' accumulation of debt as a barrier to reentry. *Journal of Law and Public Policy Clearinghouse Review, 41*(3-4), 187-197.

LIS, Inc. (2002). S*ervices for families of prison inmates.* Longmont, CO: U.S. Department of Justice, National Institute of Corrections. Retrieved October 2007, from http://www.nicic.org/pubs/2002/017272.pdf.

Lurigio, A. (2001). Effective services for parolees with mental illness. *Crime and Delinquency, 47*(3), 446-461.

Magaletta, P. R., & Herbst, D. P. (2001). Fathering from prison: Common struggles and successful solutions. *Psychotherapy, 38,* 88-96.

Malm, K., Murray, J., & Geen, R. (2006). *What About the Dads? Child welfare agencies' efforts to identify, locate and involve nonresident fathers.* Washington, D.C.: The U.S. Department of Health and Human Services, Office of the Assistant Secretary for Planning and Evaluation. Retrieved August 26, 2008, from http://aspe.hhs.gov/hsp/06/CW%2Dinvolve%2Ddads/in dex.htm.

Markman, H. J., Eason, J. A., & Grant, R. (2005). *Doing time: PREP inside and out.* Paper presented at the Smart Marriages Conference.

Martin S. S., Butzin C. A., Saum, C. A., & Inciardi, J. A. (1999). Three-year outcomes of therapeutic community treatment for drug-involved offenders in Delaware: From prison to work release to aftercare. *Prison Journal, 79,* 294–320.

McLoyd, V. C. (1998). Socioeconomic disadvantage and children development. *American Psychologist, 53*(2), 185-204.

Meek, R. (2007). Parenting education for young fathers in prison. *Child and Family Social Work, 12,* 239-247.

Mosley, J., & Thomson, E. (1995). Fathering behavior and child outcomes: The role of race and poverty. In W. Marsiglio (Ed.), *Fatherhood: Contemporary theory, research, and social policy* (pp. 148-165). Thousand Oaks, CA: Sage Publications.

Mumola, C. (1999). *Substance abuse and treatment, State and Federal prisoner, 1997.* Washington, DC: Bureau of Justice Statistics.

Mumola, C. (2000). Incarcerated parents and their children. *Bureau of Justice Statistics Special Report.* Washington, DC: Bureau of Justice Statistics.

Mumola, C. (2006). Presentation for the NIDA Research Meeting *Children of Parents in the Criminal Justice System: Children at Risk.*

Murray, J., & Farrington, D. P. (2005). Parental imprisonment: Effects on boys' antisocial behaviour and delinquency through the life-course. *Journal of Child Psychology and Psychiatry, 46*(12), 1269-1278.

Murray, J., & Farrington, D. P. (2006). Evidence-based programs for children of prisoners. *Criminology and Public Policy, 5*(4), 72 1-735.

Murray, J., Janson, C. G., & Farrington, D. P. (2007). Crime in adult offspring of prisoners. *Criminal Justice and Behavior, 34*(1), 133-149.

Naser, R., & Farrell, J. (2004). Family. In C. Visher, N. G. LaVigne, & J. Travis (Eds.), *Returning home: Understanding the challenges of prisoner reentry, Maryland pilot study: Findings from Baltimore* (pp. 103-125). Washington, DC: Urban Institute. Retrieved October 1, 2007, from http://www.urban.org/publications/410974.html.

Nelson, M., Deess, P., & Allen, C. (1999). *The first month out: Post-incarceration experiences in New York City.* New York: Vera Institute.

Nord, C. W., Brimhall, D., & West, J. (1997). *Father's involvement in schools.* Washington, DC: U.S. Department of Education.

Nurse, A. M. (2002). *Fatherhood arrested: Parenting from within the Juvenile Justice System.* Nashville, TN: Vanderbilt University Press.

Nurse, A. M. (2004). Returning to strangers: Newly paroled young fathers and their children. In M. Pattillo, D. Weiman, & B. Western (Eds.), *Imprisoning America: The social effects of mass incarceration* (pp. 76-96). New York: Russell Sage Foundation.

Office of Child Support Enforcement (OCSE), (2006), *Incarceration, Reentry and Child Support Issues: National and State Research Overview.* Washington, D.C.: U.S. Department of Health and Human Services. http://www.acf.hhs.gov/programs/cse/pubs/2006/report s/incarceration_report. pdf

Office of Child Support Enforcement (OCSE), (2006), *Working with Incarcerated and Released Parents: Lessons from OCSE grants and State Programs.* Washington, D.C.: U.S. Department of Health and Human Services. http://www.acf.hhs.gov/programs/cse/pubs/2006/guides/working_with_incarc erated _ resource _guide. pdf

O'Farrell, T. J., Murphy, C. M., Stephan, S. H., Fals-Stewart, W., & Murphy, M. (2004). Partner violence before and after couples-based alcoholism treatment for male alcoholic patients: The role of treatment involvement and abstinence. *Journal of Consulting and Clinical Psychology, 72*(2), 202-217.

Osborne, C., & McLanahan, S. (2007). *Partnership instability and child well-being.* Working Papers 946. Princeton University Center for Research on Child Wellbeing.

Page, M. & Stevens, A. H. (2004). The economic consequence of absent parents. *Journal of Human Resources, 39*(1), 80-107.

Palm, G. (2001). Parent education for incarcerated fathers. In J. Fagan & A. J. Hawkins (Eds.), *Clinical and educational interventions with fathers* (pp. 117-141). New York: The Haworth Clinical Practice Press.

Parke, M. (2003). *Are married parents really better for children? What research says about the effects of family structure on child well-being.* Couples and Marriage Series, No. 3. Washington, DC: Center for Law and Social Policy.

Parke, R. D., & Clarke-Stewart, K. A. (2001). *Effects of parental incarceration on young children.* Prepared for the From Prison to Home: The Effect of Incarceration and Reentry on Children, Families and Communities Conference (January 30-31, 2002). U.S. Department of Health and Human Services, The Urban Institute.

Parke, R. D., & Clarke-Stewart, K. A. (2003). The effects of parental incarceration on children: Perspectives, promises and policies. In J. Travis & M. Waul (Eds.), *Prisoners once removed* (pp. 189-232). Washington, DC: The Urban Institute Press.

Phillips, S. D., Burns, B. J., Wagner, R. H., Kramer, T. L., Robbins, J. M. (2002). Parental incarceration among adolescents receiving mental health services. *Journal of Child and Family Studies, 11*(4), 385-399.

Phillips, S. D., Erkanli, A., Keeler, G. P., Costello, E. J., & Angold, A. (2006). Disentangling the risks: Parent criminal justice involvement and children's exposure to family risks. *Criminology and Public Policy, 5*(4), 677- 702.

Poehlmann, J. (2005). Incarcerated mothers' contact with children, perceived family relationships, and depressive symptoms. *Journal of Family Psychology, 19*(3), 350- 357.

Robbers, Monica L.P. (2005). Focus on Family and Fatherhood: Lessons from Fairfax County's Responsible Fatherhood Program for Incarcerated Dads. *Justice Policy Journal Vol. 2 No 1.*

Rossman, S. (2001). *Services integration: Strengthening offenders and families, while promoting community health and safety.* Washington, DC: Urban Institute. Retrieved October 1, 2007, from http://aspe.hhs.gov/HSP/prison2home02/Rossman .htm.

Sampson, R. J., & Laub, J. H. (1990). Crime and deviance over the life course: The salience of adult social bonds. *American Sociological Review, 55,* 609-627.

Sampson, R. J., Laub, J. H., & Wimer, C. (2006). Does marriage reduce crime? A counterfactual approach to within-individual casual effects. *Criminology, 44*(3), 465- 508.

Sampson, R. J., Raudenbush, S. W., & Earls, F. (1997). Neighborhoods and violent crime: A multilevel study of collective efficacy. *Science, 277,* 918-924.

Schmitzer, C. (1999). Making families whole. *Family and Corrections Network Report, 20,* 12-13.

Seeman, T. E. (1996). Social ties and health: The benefits of social integration. *Annals of Epidemiology, 6,* 442-551.

Seiter, R. P., & Kadela, K. R. (2003). Prisoner reentry: What works, what does not, and what is promising. *Crime and Delinquency, 49.*

Shapiro, C. (1999). *Integrating family-focused interventions into the Criminal Justice System.* New York: Vera Institute of Justice. Retrieved November 13, 2007, from http://www.vera.org/publication_pdf/bodega_family.pdf.

Schoenborn, C. (2004). Marital status and health: United States, 1999-2002. *Advance Data from Vital Statistics. No. 351.* Hyattsville, MD: National Center for Health Statistics, Centers for Disease Control and Prevention, U.S. Department of Health and Human Services. Retrieved October 10, 2007, from http://www.cdc.gov/nchs/data/ ad/ad351.pdf

Showalter, D. & Jones, C. W. (1980). Marital and family counseling in prisons. *Social Work, 25,* 224-228.

Skarupski, K. A., Bullock, C. J., Fitch, C., Johnson, A. L., Kelso, L. M., Fox, E. R., et al. (2003). *Outcomes evaluation of the Long Distance Dads© Program.* Report to the Pennsylvania Commission on Crime and Delinquency. Retrieved November 12, 2007, from http://www.pccd.state.pa.us/pccd/lib/pccd/stats/ldd_outcomes_ final_report.pdf

Stanton, A. (1980). *When mothers go to jail.* New York: Lexington Books.

Steurer, S. J., & Smith, L. G. (2003). *Education reduces crime: Three-state recidivism study: Executive summary.* Correctional Education Association and Management and Training Corporation Institute. Retrieved from http://www.ceanational.org/ documents/3StateFinal.pdf.

Sullivan, E., Mino, M., Nelson, K., & Pope, J. (2002). *Families as a resource in recovery from drug abuse: An evaluation of La Bodega de la Familia.* New York: Vera Institute of Justice.

Tilley, D. S., & Brackley, M. (2005). Men who batter intimate partners: A grounded theory study of the development of male violence in intimate partner relationships. *Issues in Mental Health Nursing, 26,* 281-297.

Travis, J., McBride, E. C., & Solomon, A. L. (2003). *Families left behind: The hidden costs of incarceration and reentry.* Washington, DC: Urban Institute, Justice Policy Center.

Travis, J., McBride, E. C., & Solomon, A. L. (2005). *Families left behind: The hidden costs of incarceration and reentry.* Retrieved October 1, 2007, from http://www.urban.org/ publications/310882 .html.

Travis, J., Solomon, A., & Waul, M. (2001). *From prison to home: The dimensions and consequences of prisoner reentry.* Washington, DC: Urban Institute.

Visher, C. A., Knight, C. R., Chalfin, A., Roman, J. K. (forthcoming). *The impact of marital and relationship status on social outcomes for returning prisoners.* Washington, DC: Urban Institute.

Visher, C. A., & Courtney, S. M. E. (2007). *One year out: Experiences of prisoners returning to Cleveland.* Washington, DC: Urban Institute. Retrieved October 1, 2007, from http://www.urban.org/UploadedPDF/ 311445_ One_Year. pdf.

Visher, C. A., & Travis, J. (2003). Transitions from prison to community: Understanding individual pathways. *Annual Review of Sociology, 29,* 89-113.

Visher, C. A., Baer, D., & Naser, R. (2006). *Ohio prisoners' reflections on returning home.* Washington, DC: Urban Institute.

Western, B. (2004). *Incarceration, marriage, and family life.* Princeton, NJ: Princeton University Department of Sociology.

Western, B., & Beckett, K. (1999). How unregulated is the U.S. labor market? The penal system as a labor market institution. *The American Journal of Sociology,* 104 (4), 1030-1060.

Western, B., Lopoo, L., & McLanahan, S. (2004). Incarceration and the bonds between parents in fragile families. In M. Patillo, D. Weiman, and B. Western (Eds.), *Imprisoning American: The social effects of mass incarceration* (pp. 2 1-45). New York: Russell Sage Press.

Western, B., & McLanahan, S. (2000). Fathers behind bars: The impact of incarceration on family formation. *Families, Crime and Criminal Justice, 2,* 309-324.

Whelan, R. (1993). *Broken homes and battered children: A study of the relationship between child abuse and family type.* London: Family Education Trust.

# INDEX

## A

abstinence, 113
abusive, 29, 48
academic, 8, 33
access, 52, 74, 96
accountability, 48
ACF, 66
achievement, 8
adaptability, 66
adaptation, 97
addiction, 80
adjustment, 8, 34, 40, 66, 79, 97, 105, 107, 109
administration, 41
adolescents, 28, 33, 39, 113
adult, 11, 21, 53, 76, 112, 114
adults, 11, 33, 34, 38, 40
African American, 3, 15, 22, 28, 31, 37, 47
African Americans, 22
age, x, 12, 13, 15, 16, 22, 33, 34
aggression, 4, 33, 39, 54, 63
alcohol, 8, 19, 46, 47, 78, 105, 109
alcohol use, 78
alcoholism, 113
alienation, 74
anger, 3, 24, 27, 46, 48, 49, 70, 71, 96
anger management, 48, 49, 70, 96
antisocial behavior, 33
antisocial behaviour, 111

## B

anxiety, 4, 32, 39
arrest, xi, 14, 19, 26, 27, 28, 31, 32, 35, 38, 41, 56, 59, 73, 79, 80, 97, 109
assertiveness, 62
assessment, 41, 68
asymmetry, 48
atmosphere, 74, 75
attachment, 12, 24, 32, 58
attitudes, xi, 4, 20, 43, 62, 70, 71, 73, 89, 107
autonomy, 26, 54
availability, 49, 87

barrier, 52, 110
barriers, x, xii, 5, 21, 51, 53, 54, 56, 76, 87, 88, 89, 90, 91, 93, 96
basic needs, 83
behavior, 11, 12, 33, 34, 35, 71, 73, 75, 86, 105, 109, 111
behavioral problems, xii, 8, 32, 39, 61, 105
beliefs, xi, 43
beneficial effect, 63
benefits, 8, 48, 63, 78, 114
birth, 22, 33, 34
blaming, 48
blood, 38
bonds, 11, 23, 26, 32, 46, 75, 114, 116
boys, 11, 33

## Q

## R

## W

wages, 23
welfare, 4, 51, 57, 77, 111
welfare system, 4, 57
wellbeing, 9, 41, 59, 84
well-being, xi, 29, 33, 39, 43, 58, 86, 96, 101, 104
Wisconsin, 92
withdrawal, 33

wives, 25, 44, 45, 63, 66, 101, 103, 106
women, xi, 9, 21, 22, 23, 24, 25, 27, 29, 43, 44, 45, 46, 47, 49, 69, 97, 98, 107, 108
workers, 57, 64
worry, 25, 26

## Y

yield, 65, 68, 84, 99
young adults, 34